WHY SHOULD I GO TO LISBON

WHY SHOULD I GO TO ↧
LISBON

THE CITY YOU DEFINITELY NEED TO
VISIT BEFORE YOU TURN 30 (OR 130)

(m)

THIS IS WHY!

If you're looking for a city that's buzzing with energy but also knows how to chill, Lisbon is calling your name. The mix of history, culture, gastronomy, sunshine, and good vibes is hard to beat.

You can spend hours walking up and down the seven hills. Yes, it involves a lot of climbing, but it's worth every second. Every corner has a story to tell, and each area has something cool: colourful buildings, tiled walls, vibrant cafés, iconic trams, and views that make you stop and stare. This city feels alive, but it doesn't get too crowded if you know where to go. Lisbon is fun without being overwhelming.

Lisbon is also more affordable than most European capitals. You can enjoy all the tasty local dishes, explore until your feet hurt, and still have money left for a rooftop cocktail or a sunset cruise on the River Tagus.

Lisbon is perfect for both a short break and a full week. There's something for every type of trip, whether you're travelling solo, with friend(s), or your family. Beaches? Only thirty minutes away. Castles and palaces? Hop on a quick train to Sintra. Or just enjoy the sun, good food, great company, and some music. It's the kind of place where every day feels like a little adventure, but without the stress.

Lisbon is beautiful, real, and never boring. This city isn't trying to impress – it just is. So, if you're planning your next escape, make it this one. Just pack a bag and go!

CONTENTS

NEIGHBOURHOODS 8
PRACTICAL INFO 12

WHEN TO TRAVEL 30
LIFE IN LISBON 40

FOOD AND DRINKS 106
GOING OUT 128

GREEN LISBON 172
OUTSIDE OF LISBON 184

SHOPPING 142

Index 188
Who made this book? 191-192

NEIGHBOURHOODS

Lisbon is divided into twenty-four *freguesias* or districts. They cover even more *bairros* or neighbourhoods. These are our favourites:

Baixa

Downtown Lisbon. Big squares, classic cafés, and grand 18th-century buildings lining the streets. Home to Rua Augusta, numerous shops, and street performers. Yes, it's touristy, but also beautiful and the perfect place to start.

Chiado

Lisbon's artsy and elegant heart: classy with a touch of flair. Full of bookshops, theatres, and stylish cafés.

Alfama

The heart and soul of historic Lisbon. Narrow streets with hidden staircases and drying laundry. It is also the home of Fado music — soulful, emotional, and full of history. Watch the sunset from a *miradouro* (viewpoint) and get lost in this maze.

Graça

Sitting on one of Lisbon's highest hills, Graça has some of the best views in the city. More local and low-key, with cool cafés, street art, and epic *miradouros*. Perfect for a slow morning or a quiet evening walk.

Mouraria

One of Lisbon's oldest and most multicultural neighbourhoods, known for

narrow alleys, Fado music, and vibrant street art.

Arroios

A multicultural hub where street art meets fun cafés. Food spots from every corner of the globe and an artsy vibe that's ever-changing.

Avenidas Novas

The polished part of the city: broad avenues, chic boutiques, and a modern feel with a hint of old-school elegance. Perfect for a coffee or a stylish brunch.

Santo Antonio

A lively mix of high-end shopping, fancy hotels, and hidden gems. Where classic Lisbon meets a modern vibe.

Príncipe Real

Trendy and green, and one of Lisbon's coolest neighbourhoods. With its leafy square, laid-back cafés, and vintage shops, it's a favourite weekend hangout.

Bairro Alto

Quiet by day, party central by night. Packed with bars and tiny clubs, and the streets are filled with people hanging out. Casual, fun, and perfect for bar hopping.

Misericórdia

The boho heart of Lisbon. Cobblestones, tiny bars, and secret viewpoints. Where the city's charm shines brightest, especially as the sun sets.

Cais do Sodré

Along the river, Cais do Sodré transformed from sketchy to cool. Home to Time Out Market, music venues, and some of the best nightlife in town. Think street food meets DJs meets neon lights.

Estrela

Calm and charming, Estrela has its iconic basilica and leafy garden. There's a slow but steady rhythm. A beautiful mix of residential peace and timeless character.

Alcântara

Alcântara mixes old warehouses with a modern vibe. Home to the trendy LX Factory, full of indie shops, rooftop bars, and the best street art. With views of the 25 de Abril Bridge, it's great for a riverside drink.

Marvila

Lisbon's up-and-coming creative district. A little off the beaten path, packed with craft breweries, art galleries, and coworking spaces. Raw, industrial, and full of potential, you'll experience Lisbon's edgy, evolving side.

Belém

Belém is relaxed, green, filled with history and is home to the original *Pastel de Belém*, the famous pastry. Riverside views, museums, gardens, and the Jerónimos Monastery: perfect for a sunny afternoon.

TRAVEL

Lisbon's city centre is relatively small. The best way to get around town is on foot. While walking, you can soak up the atmosphere, change your plan along the way or take a break in a local café whenever the mood strikes. And most importantly, Lisbon's real beauty lies in the details, like the famous *azulejos*, the intricate tiles on buildings and pavements. Walking allows you to appreciate the smallest details. But climbing the steep hills can be exhausting at times. Luckily there is also a very good network of metros, trams, buses, lifts, and ferries.

There are four different metro lines, covering the north, east, and south of the city. Trams are easy to use, running from 6.30am to 1am. Check *metrolisboa.pt* for more information.

For visiting the western parts of town, trams are the best option. The yellow tram 28 is iconic and super scenic but also packed with tourists. Use it early in the morning or try tram 12 or 24 for less tourist traffic. Buses are clean and efficient too. There are also four *elevadors*, lifts that carry you up or downhill. Three of them are the typical yellow tram lifts, Elevador da Glória, Elevador do Lavra, and Elevador da Bica. The fourth lift, the beautiful Elevador de Santa Justa, brings you from Baixa up to Chiado. It has been doing so since 1902!

You can use single tickets or purchase a 24-hour travel card. Pay contactless or use Viva Viagem Card, a reloadable card for travel on all Lisbon public transport. More information on prices and options can be found on *carris.pt*.

TRAVEL

If you purchase the Lisboa Card, public transport is covered, including tram 28 and trains to Sintra, Cascais, Azambuja, and Setúbal. It also gives you free or discounted entrance to various tourist attractions, as well as discounts at a selection of shops and restaurants. Cards are valid for 24, 48, or 72 hours. Check the different prices and purchase your card on *lisboa-card.com*.

The train network is affordable and reliable for travelling to and from towns and villages around Lisbon. For more information, check *cp.pt*. There are also five ferry routes, with three terminals in Lisbon and four on the southern banks. The ferry offers a very enjoyable mode of transport if you want to explore a bit further out of town, with the ride itself as the main attraction. Visit *ttsl.pt* for more information.

Although new cycle paths are popping up all the time, cycling in Lisbon can be challenging. Paths are not always connected, and drivers aren't accustomed to cyclists. However, it is a great mode of transport in some areas, especially along the coast. You can rent a bicycle or use Gira, Lisbon's bike-sharing system. You can choose from electric and regular bikes, with docking stations all across the city. More information can be found on *gira-bicicletasdelisboa.pt*.

You can either use traditional taxis or use one of the apps. Uber, Bolt, and FreeNow are all available in Lisbon. They tend to provide a cheaper ride, but the official taxis are regulated and safe; just make sure the meter is switched on.

TRAVEL

WHERE TO STAY

HOSTELS

Lisbon Lounge

Rua De São Nicolau 41, 1100-547 Baixa, lisbonlounge.com

This is one of our favourites. With a great design, there is a choice of double, quadruple, or dorm rooms, and they organise lots of fun activities. You can go on a surfing trip, join their tour to Sintra, go on a pub crawl, or stay and enjoy their cocktail bar. Whatever you do, you must really try Momma Lu's Portuguese and Brazilian four-course meal. Highly recommended!

Inn Possible

Rua Regedor 3, 1100 Baixa, innpossiblelisbon.com

Excellent location, extremely friendly and helpful staff, a great breakfast for only €2, a communal kitchen, lounge and TV rooms – what more do you need? From private rooms to ten-bed dorms, you will find something there to suit your needs.

Living Lounge Hostel

Rua do Crucifixo 116, 1100-185 Baixa, livingloungehostel.com

The location of this hostel is excellent, within walking distance from most major attractions. Free breakfast, a communal kitchen, a bar, and affordable local dinners create a sociable atmosphere that attracts a slightly more mature crowd.

Yes Lisbon Hostel

Rua de São Julião 148, 1100-527 Baixa, yeshostels.com

This centrally located hostel is comfortable, clean, and a great place to make new friends. The staff are very friendly, and they really go out of their way to make you feel at home. They offer walking tours, shared dinners, pub crawls, and day trips, making it perfect for solo travellers too.

Lisb'on Hostel

Rua do Ataíde 7A, 1200-034 Chiado, lisb-onhostel.com

Downtown in the historical centre, you are never far from the action when you're staying at Lisb'on. Located in a beautiful period building, they offer both double rooms and dorms. There is a garden and outdoor seating with views of the river, so you can watch the sunset during Happy Hour. They also organise surfing trips, evening tours, walking tours, and local dinners.

Sunset Destination Hostel

Estação Ferroviária do Cais do Sodré, piso Misericordia, 1200-161, destinationhostels.com

This hostel is located inside the beautiful Cais do Sodré train station. There is a choice of dorms and private bedrooms. You'll find a small, heated pool on their rooftop, from where you can watch the sunset or join in on one of their famous sunset barbecues.

Independente Príncipe Real

Rua de São Pedro de Alcântara 81, 1250-138 Misericordia, independente.eu/principe-real

From a twelve-bed dorm to a suite for two: whatever your mood and budget, you will find it here. It is both a hostel and a hotel, set in a beautiful old palace at the perfect location. It has been turned into a funky place to have a drink, enjoy a delicious dinner, sip on some cocktails, make new friends, and rest your head.

LX Hostel

Rua Rodrigues de Faria 103, 1300-501 Alcântara, lxhostel.pt

This is our favourite place to stay. Situated in the heart of LX Factory, the design is suitably cool and industrial. They offer a fantastic free breakfast as well as a bar on their rooftop. More than fifty shops and restaurants are waiting for you at LX Factory, and if you want to explore further, it's only a short train ride downtown or to the beach.

HOTELS

M'AR De AR Auria

Rua Pascoal De Melo 130-132, Arroios, 1000-237, mardearhotels.com/en/mar-de-ar-auria

A very comfortable and affordable option at a perfect, central location. The rooms are elegant and very clean and most have a seating area or a balcony. There are also indoor and outdoor lounge areas, a bar, and a small 24/7 gym.

Hotel Principe Avila

Avenida Duque de Ávila 203, 1050-082 Avenidas Novas, hotelprincipeavila.com

A modern, spotless, and welcoming hotel in a quiet area close to the Gulbenkian Modern Art Centre. With a metro station nearby, it is easy to quickly go downtown. There are single, double, and triple rooms available, as well as a bar and a very good breakfast.

Mama Shelter Lisboa

Rua Vale do Pereiro 19, 1250-009 Santo António, mamashelter.com/lisboa

Come to mama for luxury without completely blowing your budget. Quirky, beautiful and always buzzing. The beds are super comfy, and there is an all-day restaurant as well as an amazing rooftop bar. It has some of the best views of the city and the River Tagus and you don't even need to climb the hills for that reward!

↓ MAMA SHELTER LISBON

WHERE TO STAY

23

GOOD TO KNOW

Lisbon is easy to love with its sunny skies, cool neighbourhoods, and laid-back energy. But like any city, it has its own rhythms and rules. Whether it's your first time here or you're coming back for more, knowing a few local habits and practical tips can make your trip smoother and even more fun. Here's everything you should know before hitting the streets of Portugal's capital.

Water

Although tap water in Lisbon is treated and officially safe, many locals and tourists prefer bottled water. Portugal is known for its clean, top-quality spring waters with naturally high pH levels. You can find a huge variety in shops and restaurants, making it both widely available and affordable.

Language

The language in Portugal is Portuguese. Never assume you can get by in Spanish, but in most places, you can speak English. Obviously, learning a few basic words is much appreciated:
Hello = *Olá!*
Goodbye = *Adeus*
Thank you = *Obrigada*
Please = *Por favor*
Yes = *Sim*; No = *Não*

Lisboetas

Lisboetas, also called *alfacinhas* or 'little lettuces', are friendly, warm, welcoming, and not too loud. They're not the chattiest with strangers, but a smile and a simple *Olá* go a long way. Every *Lisboeta* has their favourite bakery, tram route, or viewpoint and they will defend it like it's a sports team. So now you know how to get them started ...

Local routine

Lisbon just doesn't rush. Most shops and cafés open around 9am or 10am. Mornings are calm, and the city slowly picks up speed throughout the day. Lunch is sacred: expect long lunch breaks. Many businesses close between 1pm and 3pm, especially outside the tourist zones. Locals usually eat dinner around 8pm. If you show up at a restaurant earlier, don't be surprised if it's empty or not even open yet.

Coffee culture

Lisboetas love their coffee! To start your day like a local, order a *bica* (an inky espresso) and sip it standing at the counter. Or sit down with a pastry and a *meia de leite* (espresso with warm milk) or a *galão* (with extra milk).

Dining etiquette

Meals in Lisbon are unhurried and sociable; *Lisboetas* like their *petiscos*, small dishes to share. Don't expect fast service, and don't take the waiters' pace personally. The staff are usually very friendly and relaxed. In many restaurants, waiters will bring bread, butter, cheese, or olives to the table without asking. These aren't free: you'll be charged for them. If you're not interested, just say so — this is completely normal. Tipping isn't required but always appreciated. Round up the bill or leave 5-10% for good service. In cafés, some small change is enough.

Local delicacies

Pastel de Nata, the famous custard tart: you simply can't visit Lisbon without trying this pastry. Every local has their favourite bakery so do ask around! *Ginjinha*, the city's sweet cherry liquor. It is a must-try, ideally in a tiny bar in Rossio or Alfama. It is

usually served in a shot glass, sometimes even in a chocolate cup!

Bacalhau, codfish, is served in many ways. A typical local dish is *bacalhau à bràs*, cod with scrambled eggs.

Sardinhas assadas, grilled sardines. Although some restaurants serve them all year round, it's best to enjoy them between June and October. If you get them out of season, they were likely frozen.

Ameijôas à bulhão pato, clams. This dish, usually prepared with olive oil, white wine, lemon juice, and garlic, is named after the Portuguese writer Raimundo António de Bulhão Pato.

Miradouros

Lisbon is filled with numerous *miradouros*, and these viewpoints are a big deal. They offer incredible views over the colourful houses with terracotta roofs, the river in the background, a glimpse of Ponte 25 de Abril and Cristo Rei on the other side of the river. Ideally soaked in the golden light of the sun setting, locals gather to enjoy a few drinks, watch the sunset, or simply relax. This really is the local way of life.

Dress code

Lisbon is casual, but stylish. You don't need to dress up, but locals love their clean trainers and simple looks that are well put together. Flip-flops are strictly for the beach. You will need proper shoes to climb those hills anyway.

Money

Portugal is mostly card-friendly, especially Lisbon. You can pay with your card in restaurants, shops, and even taxis. But always carry some euros just in case, especially for local markets, small bakeries or cafés, street vendors, and older shops outside the tourist zones. Cash machines (Multibanco) are everywhere but always check your bank's fees before using them.

Museums & sights

Most major attractions open around 10am and close between 5pm and 7pm. Many museums are closed on Mondays, so make sure to plan ahead. Some museums offer free entrance on the first Sunday of the month, and many offer discounts to students. Make sure to check their website for opening hours and the availability of discounted tickets. Booking your ticket in advance will often save you from queuing.

Tram 28

A ride on the yellow tram 28 is iconic and incredibly scenic but it's also packed with tourists. And pickpockets! Always keep your valuables close. Use it early in the morning or try tram 12 or 24 for less tourist traffic.

Shopping

Expect a mix of modern malls, local shops, and outdoor markets for your shopping spree. Shops usually open from 10am until 7pm or 8pm Mondays to Saturdays. Independent shops and boutiques may close for lunch. Most small businesses don't open on Sundays. Shopping malls like Colombo or Amoreiras are open daily, often until 11pm or midnight.

LISBON IN SPRING

Spring is one of the best times to visit Lisbon, when it's all about colour and calm. The weather is warm but not too hot, perfect for wandering through Alfama's alleyways or climbing to a *miradouro* (viewpoint) without getting sweaty.

The light at this time of year is golden and soft, especially in the early evening, and it makes everything look even more photogenic. Locals start spending more time outdoors, enjoying alfresco lunches, stretching out in parks, or sipping coffee by the river. There's a sense of excitement in the air, but the atmosphere is relaxed.

In May, something magical happens: the jacaranda trees bloom. These purple-bloomed giants line Lisbon's streets and parks, and when they burst into flower, it's like the city gets its own version of cherry blossom season. Pavements are covered in soft, purple petals, and the city feels enchanted. If you're into photography or just like a solid Instagram moment, this is one to catch. You'll want proof Lisbon really does look this dreamy.

If you're visiting in spring, bring layers. It can still get breezy at night, especially near the water or in higher parts of the city.

Spring is Lisbon at its most effortless: cool, calm, and impossibly charming.

LISBON IN SUMMER

Summer in Lisbon is loud, bright, and buzzing with energy. The city feels most alive on those sun-soaked days, warm nights, and a calendar packed with events. In June, it all kicks off with the city's biggest party: the Festas de Lisboa (Santo António), when the streets of Alfama explode with music, grilled sardines, colourful streamers, and people dancing till dawn. For most of the month – especially on 12th & 13th June – Alfama, Graça, and Mouraria come alive with lights, crowds, and serious party vibes. You haven't really experienced Lisbon until you've joined a street party in the summer heat. It's chaotic, fun, and totally unforgettable.

Daytime is perfect for heading to the beaches of Cascais or Costa da Caparica, or exploring the castles and palaces of Sintra. But be warned – July and August can get seriously hot, with temperatures pushing 35°C. That means early sightseeing, lots of shade, and more than one frozen drink.

In August, many locals head out of town for their own holidays. You might find some smaller shops and cafés closed, especially in the less touristy neighbourhoods, but the city doesn't slow down much. Rooftop bars, sunset views from *miradouros*, and summer music festivals keep Lisbon buzzing well into the night.

Pack light clothes, sunscreen, and a refillable water bottle – you'll need it all. Summer in Lisbon isn't always breezy, but it's bold, fun, and 100% worth it.

LISBON IN AUTUMN

Autumn in Lisbon feels like a secret season. The crowds start to thin out, but the weather stays warm well into October. It's that perfect in-between vibe: sunny days, cooler nights, and just the right amount of buzz without the chaos. The air feels lighter, and the city breathes at a slower, more comfortable pace.

There's a golden light that hits the city just right, perfect for photos and slow afternoons by the river, especially late in the afternoons. September still feels like summer – yes, beach days are still on the table – and October brings a gentle shift. Suddenly, cosy cafés and Fado music start to feel more appealing than beach towels.

It's also a great time to explore Lisbon's more low-key side. Prices drop a little compared to summer, and the slower pace makes it easier to connect with locals and discover hidden spots, like bookshops tucked behind tiled walls or rooftop bars with unbeatable views and sunny *miradouros* without a crowd. A light jacket is a must as the evenings get cooler, but by layering you can stay out all day.

If it's your first time in Lisbon, autumn might be the sweet spot – still lively, but more laid-back. You'll get a taste of everything, minus the tourist overload.

LISBON IN WINTER

Lisbon in winter is chilly but not cold by most standards. Think 10-16°C, with the occasional rainy day. You'll see locals in coats and scarves, while you might be comfortable in a light jacket. December is festive, with sparkling lights across Baixa, Christmas markets, roasted chestnuts on every corner, and a jolly atmosphere without the deep freeze.

It's a time for slower travel: enjoying a hot drink in tiled cafés, exploring museums, or listening to live Fado in intimate spaces. Museums are quieter, the streets less crowded, and there's more space to take in the city's details.
Lisbon is still very walkable in winter, and the city's hills are easier to climb without the summer heat. You'll appreciate the lack of crowds at popular spots like Belém Tower and LX Factory.

December is beautiful, but many restaurants and attractions close during the last week for the holidays; double-check opening hours before planning a big day out. January and February are budget-friendly, with cheaper flights and fewer tourists — perfect if you're travelling light and looking for local vibes. It's a great time to blend in, shop for vintage clothes, visit timeless bookshops, or finally take that long lunch without any pressure.

Winter in Lisbon isn't about hype; it's about calm, charm, and discovering the city at your own pace.

LIFE IN LISBON

HISTORY

One of the oldest cities in Europe

Lisbon's history as a city began in 205 BCE, making Lisbon one of the oldest cities in Europe. The city is built on the ruins of the Roman city Olisipo, but only the theatre and parts of the old city walls are above ground today. The theatre has been thoroughly excavated and is the central focus of Museu de Lisboa's Teatro Romano site.

Christianity also has strong roots in Lisbon, although Christians faced persecution when attempting to spread their religion. Many were martyred, most famously the three Holy Martyrs of Lisbon; three Christian siblings who travelled to Olisipo after receiving a vision from an angel. Others travelled to Olisipo for its trade. The city was famous for its *garum*, an ancient Roman fish sauce, which was exported to Rome en masse.

From Odysseus to the Moors

It's a nice legend – the Greek hero Odysseus founding Lisbon. And it might even be true; the Latin names for Odysseus and Lisbon, Ulysses and Ulyssipo, are strikingly similar. As is often the case with legends, the story has some grains of truth. Around 1200 BCE, Phoenicians, seafarers – just like Odysseus – sailed from what is now known as Syria and Lebanon. They formed a settlement where you can now find the city with 3 million of *Lisboetas*. A thousand years later, the Romans conquered this settlement and made it into a city. After the fall of the Roman Empire, the city was invaded and conquered numerous times by multiple Germanic tribes. Eventually, the Moors settled in Lisbon (and other large parts of Europe), which they turned back into a centre for trade, as it had been during the Roman occupation. Trade was conducted with virtually the entire Islamic world, which helped grow the city into one of the largest in Europe. The Moors, like the Romans, also added onto the city walls, which are visible to this day.

Reconquista

The Reconquista ('reconquest') was a Christian European military operation to regain control of the Iberian Peninsula from the Islamic Moors. The Reconquista in Portugal lasted nearly 400 years. It required many troops, namely knights and Templars (Christian soldiers), and led to the creation of the Portuguese marines – one of the world's oldest. In 1128, the kingdom of Portugal separated itself from Spain, with Afonso I crowned as its first king. During his reign, a Christian edifice that had been converted into a mosque by the Moors, was turned into a cathedral. After another 364 years, all the Muslim territory on the Iberian Peninsula was finally reconquered.

Colonisation

The Portuguese were at the forefront of the Age of Discovery, with Vasco da Gama as the first to travel around the entirety of Africa, and Pedro Álvares Cabral the first European to set foot in Brazil. The Treaty of Tordesillas split the globe in two, with one half belonging to Portugal and the other to Spain. The line dividing the globe was meant to give the Spanish the entirety of the Americas, however, the easternmost part of Brazil crossed past that line, meaning it belonged to the Portuguese. This is why Brazil to this day is the only Portuguese-speaking country in either of the Americas. Some historians

believe that the Portuguese knew about the Brazilian landmass before the treaty was signed, and that Cabral's landing in Brazil only a few years later was no accident. Portugal had fewer large colonies than other European countries but instead had many smaller settlements and forts all along the African and Asian coastlines. However, the country did still colonise modern-day Brazil, Timor-Leste, Angola, Guinea-Bissau, Senegal, and Mozambique. Some of the smaller settlements include Macau (which was only handed back to China in 1999), Madeira, and Nagasaki.

Birth of Pastéis de nata

When you think of pastries in Lisbon, you'll probably think of *pastéis de nata*. The small custard-and-puff-pastry *pastel* was invented in the 18th century by monks in the Jerónimos monastery in Belém. The monks used egg whites to starch their clothes, and ended up with an abundance of egg yolks, which they disposed of by making pastries. Now, the *pastéis* are so famous that every day at least 4,000 people queue to try them. Find the best spots for getting some on page 112.

Earthquake of 1755

In 1755, an earthquake in the Atlantic Ocean with a magnitude of at least 7.7 on the Richter scale sent massive shockwaves to Lisbon. Combined with the ensuing tsunami and fires, it nearly destroyed the entirety of the city. Around 85 per cent of the buildings were destroyed and a lot of art and historical records were lost. At Quake, you can experience what this might have been like (see page 64). After the earthquake, King Joseph I developed an intense fear of being surrounded by walls, so it wasn't until after his death that the construction of a new royal palace was started. To avoid another event causing similar destruction, the Pombaline style of architecture was developed. Buildings would now be made of materials that could move with a quake, which would prevent collapse. During the reconstruction of the city, more room was left for light and openness, which sets Lisbon apart from other medieval cities.

Azulejos – the famous tiles

Also typical of Lisbon are the gorgeous façades covered in blue tiles, *azulejos*. These tiles were introduced by the Moors, who decorated their palaces in the 15th century using them both inside and out. *Azulejos* also became part of the Pombaline style of architecture, often featuring historical or biblical images. If you're going to take the metro, you'll almost certainly see some, as the city has been commissioning *azulejos* from various artists since 1988. If you're in the area, the tiles at Parque station are definitely worth a look; they intricately depict Portuguese sea voyages and history.

Estado Novo

Portugal remained a monarchy until 1908, when Carlos I was assassinated in Lisbon. This event led to the establishment of the First Portuguese Republic, which was in place for just sixteen years and was eventually replaced by Estado Novo (the Second Portuguese Republic, literally meaning 'New State'). Estado Novo was a dictatorial regime that would last until the 1974 Carnation Revolution. During this reign, the government promoted a nationalist architectural style that would later be known as Portuguese Suave. A famous example of this style is the monument to the Portuguese

Age of Discovery in Belém, built during the 1940 World Expo. It features various icons from Portuguese history, with Henry the Navigator at the forefront. When other European countries started the process of decolonisation, António de Oliveira Salazar (then prime minister of Portugal) made a staunch effort to retain the Portuguese colonies. This led to the Portuguese Colonial War, which was a combination of various uprisings and conflicts in Angola, Mozambique, and Guinea-Bissau during a thirteen-year period, from 1961 until the end of the Estado Novo regime.

Portuguese Jews

Although the Jewish community in Lisbon wasn't formally recognised until 1913, its Jewish population is significant. In 1496, the Edict of Expulsion forced all Jews out of the predominantly Christian country. But after they were allowed back at around 1800, the Jewish community flourished. In 1904, the Lisbon Synagogue was the first to be built in Portugal. Even though Portugal granted many transit visas during the Second World War, unfortunately not many permanent visas were awarded to Jewish refugees. Their Lisbon community currently is small, but tight-knit and many community programs are still active.

Futebol: one city, six clubs

Since the first organised game of football took place in 1875, Portugal has been football-crazy, and Lisbon is no exception. The city is home to two of the 'Big Three' Portuguese clubs (Sport Lisboa e Benfica, and Sporting Clube de Portugal) and even has four more. Many world-famous players made their start in Lisbon, including Cristiano Ronaldo and Eusébio. Lisbon's strong tradition of developing sports talent from a young age through various programs and academies helps with the proliferation of football culture and clubs in the city. A match worth seeing is Benfica vs. Sporting CP, as the fierce rivalry between the clubs makes each game interesting.

World Expo 1998

In 1998, exactly 500 years after Da Gama arrived in India, the World Expo took place in Lisbon. Along the Tagus, many of the buildings commissioned for use at the Expo, such as the Gare do Oriente and the Casino Lisboa, are still in use. About one-third of the designated space consists of parks, so you'll also find some nature. After the Expo ended in 1998, those buildings were either converted and became malls or museums, or were sold to companies as office space, which helped raise funds to host the Expo. The modern design, combined with the Expo itself, brought new interest into the eastern part of the city, and street artist Bordalo II placed one of his giant installations made from recycled waste in the district.

SIGHTSEEING

Miradouros

*Largo Portas do Sol,
1100-411 Alfama*

Lisbon is built on seven hills, there are viewpoints — *miradouros* — wherever you turn. Miradouro de Santa Luzia is one of Lisbon's most popular viewpoints for a reason. It is covered with grapevines providing respite from the sun, and it offers amazing views towards the River Tagus, the São Vicente de Fora church, and the buildings of Alfama. You'll probably spot some cruise ships too. It can get crowded, so try to visit either early or late. Miradouro das Portas do Sol is just a short walk from there. It often attracts fewer people and the view of Alfama is equally stunning, particularly at sunrise. Miradouro de São Pedro de Alcântara is arguably the most beautiful viewpoint. It offers a breathtaking view of Lisbon's colourful skyline, overlooked by the impressive Castelo de São Jorge. It's magical at sunset. Finally, Miradouro da Graça is a popular gathering spot. It has great views of the city, from the castle all the way up to the river, with trees providing some welcome shade. It is a great place to watch the sun set over the castle.

Praça do Comércio

*Praça do Comércio,
1100-148 Baixa*

Also known as Terreiro do Paço, Praça do Comércio is one of Lisbon's most iconic sights. It lies between the River Tagus and Rua da Augusta,

Lisbon's famous pedestrian street. It is one of the largest squares in Portugal, and is surrounded by impressive government buildings, shops, and restaurants. In the middle of the square stands a statue of King Jose I, which was erected in 1775.

Arco da Rua Augusta

Praça do Comércio, 1100-148 Baixa

This arch was built to commemorate Lisbon's reconstruction after the 1755 earthquake. You can climb to the top for a bird's-eye view over Praça do Comércio, the river and the city. From here, you can stroll along Rua Augusta.

Sé de Lisboa

Largo da Sé, 1100-585 Alfama, sedelisboa.pt

Located in the Alfama district, Sé de Lisboa is the oldest building and is Lisbon's only cathedral. After many renovations throughout the centuries, the cathedral is made up of several architectural styles, including Neoclassical, Baroque, Roman, and Gothic. It stands twelve metres tall and makes an impressive sight with its towers and the attached 16th-century medieval monastery.

Castelo de São Jorge

Rua de Santa Cruz do Castelo, 1100-129 Alfama, castelodesaojorge.pt

This castle, perched on the highest of the seven hills, has been a site of fortifications for centuries. This is the restored version of the 11th-century Moorish construction, which largely collapsed in the 1755 earthquake. It is an interesting historical site, museum, and national monument, but it offers 360-degree vistas of the city and the Tagus too. It is also home to a group of peacocks. Make sure to buy your tickets in advance as the queues can get long.

Panteão Nacional

*Campo de Santa Clara,
1100-471 Alfama,
panteaonacional.gov.pt*

This bright white building houses the tombs of national greats such as Benfica's all-time top scorer Eusébio and Fado singer Amália Rodrigues. The dome, which you will spot from far away, seems to touch the sky. The view from the terrace is breathtaking.

Igreja de São Roque

*Largo Trindade Coelho,
1200-470 Bairro Alto,
museusaoroque.scml.pt*

The exterior of this church is not especially striking. But inside, a world of delight is waiting to be discovered. It was the first Jesuit church in Portugal and among one of the first in the world. It served as the society's base in Portugal for over two hundred years, until the Jesuits were expelled. Visits to the church are free; the adjoining museum charges a fee.

Palácio da Ajuda

*Largo da Ajuda, 1349-021
Ajuda,
palacioajuda.gov.pt*

When the royal family's residence on the waterfront was destroyed in the 1755 earthquake, they decided to relocate to a site higher up. It was going to be one of the largest palaces in Europe, but because of invasions and changing politics they never built more than one-fifth of the structure originally planned. Visit it to see how Portuguese royalty lived. This palace has it all, the chandeliers, ballrooms, and gold-trimmed everything — and it is still low-key enough to explore at your leisure.

Mosteiro dos Jerónimos

Praça do Império, 1400-206 Belém, jeronimosmonastery-tickets.com

This monastery is a UNESCO World Heritage Site and one of Portugal's crown jewels. It was commissioned in 1501 by King Manuel I to celebrate Vasco da Gama's successful voyage to India. It was completed in 1601, and it is breathtaking. Walking through it feels like entering a fantasy novel. With massive stone arches and detailed carvings, the weight of history is palpable throughout.

Torre de Belém

Avenida Brasília, 1400-038 Belém, torrebelem.com

This watchtower was built on the banks of the Tagus in the 16th century to protect the harbour. This masterpiece, covered in lavish decorations, is still in excellent condition. Originally built to keep an eye on enemies approaching from the water, Torre de Belém became a monument to the many successful Portuguese voyages of discovery – though these are not without controversy today. For a long time, the tower also served as a prison. It has been on the UNESCO World Heritage List since 1983.

Cristo Rei

Alto do Pragal, Avenida Cristo Rei, 2800-058 Almada, cristorei.pt

The Christ the King statue, *Cristo Rei*, stands over a hundred metres tall. The Lisbon landmark on the banks of the Tagus extends its arms to embrace the city. The statue was commissioned by Portuguese dictator António de Oliveira Salazar and completed in 1959. It was modelled after the famous statue in Rio de Janeiro. To get there, take the ferry from the Cais do Sodré district to Cacilhas, and then take the 3001 bus. It is usually fairly quiet, but the view is phenomenal.

MUSEUMS & GALLERIES

Lisbon Story Centre

Terreiro do Paço 78-81, 1100-148 Baixa, lisboastorycentre.pt

This interactive museum tells Lisbon's entire history in about an hour with audio guides, projections, and even a mini earthquake experience. Fun, fast, and full of surprises.

Museum of Design and Fashion (MUDE)

Rua Augusta 24, 1100-053 Baixa, mude.pt

MUDE showcases everything from iconic fashion pieces to wild furniture designs. Each one more stylish than the last. It's a top pick for creative inspiration.

Carmo Archeological Museum

Largo do Carmo, 1200-092 Chiado, museuarqueologico docarmo.pt

What's better than a museum in a roofless Gothic church? This place is all ruins and vibes, with ancient artefacts; one of the most Instagrammable spots in the city. It's the kind of place where history feels tic, especially at sunset.

Fado Museum

Largo de Chafariz de Dentro 1, 1100-139 Alfama, museudofado.pt

Even if you've never heard of Fado, this place will have you feeling all the feels. Learn how Portugal's most emotional music started in the backstreets of Lisbon and why it's still relevant today.

Museu Nacional do Azulejo

Rua Madre Deus 4, 1900-312 Beato, museunacionaldoazulejo.pt

In this tile museum, you'll see how Lisbon's most iconic art form evolved from medieval mosaics to modern street style. Plus, it's housed in a former convent, so the surroundings are gorgeous too. Their café is absolutely beautiful.

Calouste Gulbenkian Museum

Avenida de Berna 45A, 1067-001 Avenidas Novas, gulbenkian.pt

This is Lisbon's top-tier classical art museum. You'll find all sorts of Egyptian, Syrian, Chinese, and Japanese artefacts, and much more. Although its historical provenance may raise eyebrows, it is one of the best private art collections in the world.

Calouste Gulbenkian Museum – Modern Collection

Rua Dr. Nicolau de Bettencourt, 1050-078 Avenidas Novas, gulbenkian.pt

The Gulbenkian's cooler, modern little sibling. Think Portuguese 20th century art, experimental pieces, and a peaceful garden that feels like a hidden chill-out zone. Great for a calm afternoon.

↓ CARMO ARCHEOLOGICAL MUSEUM

Museu de Medeiros e Almeida

Rua Rosa Araújo 41, 1250-194 Santo António, museumedeirosealmeida.pt

Visiting this museum is like stepping into a time capsule: it's packed with vintage furniture, clocks, and glam décor. If you're into vintage aesthetics, interiors, or just fancy looking around someone's mansion – go!

National Museum of Natural History and Science

Rua da Escola Politécnica, Príncipe Real, museus.ulisboa.pt

This museum is a treasure for curious minds. Located in the elegant Príncipe Real neighbourhood, it offers a mix of classic and contemporary exhibits. Explore everything from dinosaur fossils and mineral collections to interactive science displays. The attached Botanical Garden is a serene spot, perfect for a pleasant stroll among exotic plants.

Galeria Zé dos Bois (ZDB)

Rua da Barroca 59, 1200-047 Bairro Alto, zedosbois.org

ZDB is one of Lisbon's hottest art spaces, hidden away in Bairro Alto's maze of streets. Housed in an 18th-century palace, it hosts edgy exhibitions, experimental concerts, and creative workshops. A real hub for the city's alternative scene.

National Museum of Ancient Art

Rua das Janelas Verdes 17, 1249-017 Santos, museudearteantiga.pt

Old-school but gold. This museum is filled with paintings and religious art. If you're into Renaissance, it's a must. Also: great river views from their garden café.

B-MAD Bernardo Museum of Art Deco

Rua 1.º de Maio 24, 1300-474 Alcântara, bmad.pt

Get ready for a trip back in time at B-MAD, an Art Deco and Art Nouveau wonderland tucked inside a gorgeous 18th-century palace. From stylish furniture and quirky glass art to glittering silverware, everything is a treat for design lovers and curious minds alike. And as a sweet bonus your visit ends with a free wine tasting in the garden.

MACAM – Museu de Arte Contemporânea Armando Martins

Rua da Junqueira 66, 1300-343 Alcântara–Belém, macam.pt

Brand new and buzzing, MACAM is a contemporary art museum that feels like an art-infused escape. Housed in a lavishly restored palace, it blends galleries with a garden, a bar inside a chapel, and even hotel rooms decked out in modern masterpieces. Pop by for an exhibit or stay for the ultimate artsy sleepover.

Underdogs Gallery

Rua Fernando Palha 56, 1950-132 Marvila, under-dogs.net

Underdogs is Lisbon's urban art HQ, featuring work from big name graffiti artists and rising local talent. Expect bold, political, and offbeat exhibitions. Founded by local artist Vhils in 2013, Underdogs began as a project to showcase graffiti and urban artists in a gallery setting.

Pavilhão do Conhecimento

Largo José Mariano Gago 1, 1990-073 Parque das Nações, pavconhecimento.pt

Portugal's best science museum. Think experiments, illusions, and exhibits you are allowed to touch. Fun whether you're 8 or 28. There's also a climbing wall.

↓ MUDE – MUSEUM OF DESIGN AND FASHION

MAAT

Avenida Brasília, 1300-598 Belém, maat.pt

Not your average museum — at MAAT, future ideas meet good design. The building looks like a spaceship on the river, and inside, you'll find modern art, bold design, and tech exhibits. The rooftop view is also a total bonus.

MAC/CCB

Praça do Império, 1449-003 Belém, ccb.pt

Part of the huge cultural hub at Centro Cultural de Belém, MAC/CCB has contemporary art, design, and architecture under one roof. It's home to big names like Picasso and Warhol, plus lots of Portuguese artists, set in a modern riverside building in historic Belém.

Berardo Collection Museum

Praça do Império, 1449-003 Belém, berardocollection.com

A massive collection of contemporary art inside Centro Cultural de Belém. From Warhol and Picasso to Portuguese legends, this museum covers the biggest names in modern art. Bonus: it's free on most days!

Quake – Lisbon Earthquake Museum

Rua Cais da Alfândega Velha, 39, 1300-598 Belém, lisbonquake.com

Part immersive experience, part high-tech museum, Quake covers the 1755 Lisbon earthquake. Escape room meets time travel — don't expect a history lecture. Walk through recreated streets, feel the simulated tremors, and come out with a whole new appreciation for how the city was rebuilt. Educational, but also seriously fun.

Museu dos Coches

Praça Areeiro 6, 1300-504 Belém, museudoscoches-ipmuseus.pt

Don't let the name fool you. This place is cooler than it sounds. You'll see royal carriages from centuries ago that look like something out of Bridgerton. It's strangely fascinating.

MAAT – MUSEUM OF ART, ARCHITECTURE AND TECHNOLOGY

STREET ART

In recent years, Lisbon has become one of the global capitals of urban art. Of course, there is an ongoing battle with less skilled taggers leaving their marks all over town. At the same time, the city is slowly becoming an open-air museum of incredible urban art. Hunting for street art tends to bring you to the more creative outskirts of a city: it is the perfect way to go off the beaten path. Most artworks are neither enclosed nor protected, so double-check if a work you'd like to see still exists. You can use an app like Street Art Cities or join a street art tour to make sure you'll see the best pieces.

Alfama

You'll find the History of Lisbon Mural inside a tunnel underneath Miradouro das Portas do Sol in Alfama. Painted by Nuno Saraiva in a comic book style, it depicts the history of Lisbon. It covers historical events such as the Portuguese Inquisition, the 1755 earthquake, and the 1974 Carnation Revolution. Despite continuously being the target of vandalism, this mural is still spectacular.

Graça

Some world-famous street artists have created pieces in Graça. Let's start with Shepard Fairey, a.k.a. OBEY. Yes, he also founded that fashion label. Fairey's mural on Rua Natália Correia is a tribute to Portugal's Carnation Revolution. It shows a woman in a revolutionary beret holding a machine gun with a flower in its barrel. It is the first thing you'll see when you walk from Alfama into Graça. It is a reminder of the country's revolutionary history and the embodiment of the power of non-violent protest. His iconic Obama *HOPE* poster (2008) is still his most famous work, but *Peace Guard* is just as iconic.

In Rua da Graça, you'll find the colourful mural *Fado tropical em tons RGB* ('Tropical Fado in RGB shades'). It was created by Portuguese artist OzeArv.

The corner of Sapadores and Rua Natália Correia houses the iconic mural *Era Uma Vez*, 'Once Upon a Time', by Lisbon-born Isa Silva.

Vhils, aka Alexandre Farto, is the founder of the Underdogs Gallery in Marvila. He is a Portuguese artist known for creating portraits by using 'creative destruction', as he calls it. He seeks to uncover the invisible that lies beneath the surface by cutting, carving, drilling, etching, and blasting his way through layers of materials. One of our favourites is his collaborative piece with OBEY at 39 Rua da Senhora da Glória. This mural features a woman's face split between Fairey's and Vhils' distinctive styles. And these are just a few examples. Go and explore for more!

Mouraria

The multicultural neighbourhood of Mouraria is full of colour and art. If you wander down Escadinhas de São Cristóvão, you will discover some beautiful works. Make your way to the car park by Castelo de São Jorge, and you'll see some of the finest work by Portuguese street artists.

Arroios

At the heart of this neighbourhood, you will find a food market in a square decorated by the art collective Boa Hora. In 2012, the city council commissioned them to create a space aimed at people instead of cars, which resulted in this colourful floor art. In the same area, you can spot artworks by the Ukrainian duo Interesni Kazki and Portuguese artist Akacorleone.

Marvila

Lisbon's up-and-coming creative district is raw, industrial, and filled with street art. Fábrica Braço de Prata, an old weapons factory, is one of most creative spaces in the city. Its walls are covered with murals.

In this part of town, you can also find the Underdogs Gallery and 8 Marvila, both great hunting grounds for street art.

Marvila's own LS painted a stunning female portrait with a reference to the famous Portuguese Azulejos. His work can also be found along the platforms of the Marvila train station. Go out to see how many more you can spot!

CINEMA

Although film titles in Portugal are usually translated, the films themselves are not dubbed. They're almost always shown in their original language.

Cinema Ideal

Rua do Loreto 15,
1200-241 Chiado,
cinemaidealemcasa.pt

This tiny cinema is the oldest in Portugal that is still operating. Since opening in 1904, it has served many different audiences. Before its rescue ten years ago, it showed porn films for three decades, while the building slowly deteriorated. It was finally transformed into one of the best spots for independent cinema.

Cinemateca Portuguesa – Museu do Cinema

Rua Barata Salgueiro, 39,
1269-059 Santo António,
cinemateca.pt

Dive into the former glamour of the film industry. Cinemateca not only provides screenings and film festivals, but also houses a museum, bookshop, and restaurant.

Medeia Monumental Cinema

Avenida 5 de Outubro 42,
1050-083 Campo Grande,
medeiafilmes.com/
cinemas/cinema-medeia-
nimas

This cinema steers clear of the mainstream, showing rare and unusual classics and arthouse films. Tucked away in the Monumental building near Saldanha, this fifty-year old cinema has a nostalgic charm with just the right dose of retro cool.

Cine Society

tickets.cinesociety.pt

This open-air cinema offers both classic and contemporary films at unique locations with amazing views over the city. Screenings pop up on rooftops and public squares during the summer months. Grab some popcorn, cuddle up, and enjoy Lisbon's funnest movie night.

↓ CINE SOCIETY

FESTIVALS

Moda Lisboa – Lisbon Fashion Week

Lisbon's fashion scene goes into full catwalk mode in March and October, with incredible designers, streetwear, and bold looks. Even if you don't manage to score an invite, there usually are public events as well as pop-ups that are worth checking out.

modalisboa.pt

Indie Lisboa – International Independent Film Festival

Perfect for discovering weird, wonderful indie films from around the world. There are usually youth screenings, there are lots of parties, and a very laid-back crowd. It's all about creativity and new voices in cinema. Held in April and May.

indielisboa.com

ARCO – Contemporary Art Fair

A massive fair in May, showcasing modern and contemporary art by Portuguese and international artists. Great for inspiration (or daydreaming about buying a €10,000 painting).

ifema.es/en/arco

Santo António / Festas de Lisboa

The ultimate Lisbon experience. Every June, the city turns into a massive block party celebrating Santo António, Lisbon's patron saint (and matchmaker, apparently). Expect grilled sardines, colourful streamers, music blasting from every alley, and the wildest street parties in Alfama and beyond. It's messy, loud, and 100% unforgettable.

Rock in Rio – Lisboa

The Lisbon edition of Brazil's famous Rock in Rio is a giant festival-meets-theme-park. Big pop and rock acts, rides, food zones, and crowds ready to go all out. Every two years in June in Parque da Bela Vista.

rockinriolisboa.pt

NOS Alive

One of Europe's top music festivals, NOS Alive brings massive international headliners (past performers included Arctic Monkeys, Billie Eilish, and The Strokes) to the Lisbon coast. Three days of sun, sea, and live music in Algés, just outside the city. In July.

nosalive.com

Super Bock Super Rock

Another big-name music festival in July – Charlotte de Witte being one of their past performers – this festival leans more towards rock, indie, and alt-rap vibes. The crowd is a little edgier, the beer is always cold, and it usually takes place in Parque das Nações or sometimes down south.

superbocksuperrock.pt

Alkantara Festival

A celebration of contemporary dance, theatre, and performance, often very experimental and international. If you're into avant-garde performances or want to see something unexpected, this is your scene. Takes place in November.

alkantara.pt

LEFFEST – Lisboa film Festival

For the film lovers: a serious but stylish festival in November, showing international cinema, documentaries, and classics, often with Q&As and guest directors.

leffest.com

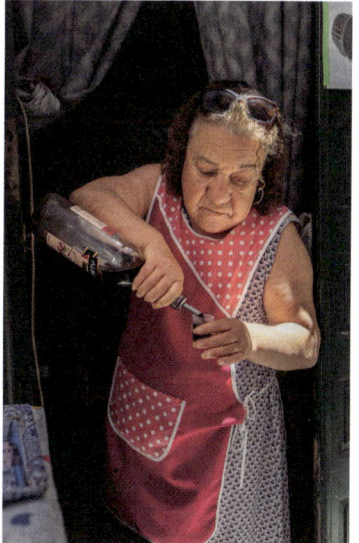

THINGS TO DO

Theatre

Lisbon has a vibrant theatre scene. The 1793 Teatro Nacional de São Carlos was classed as a National Monument in 1996. It's a great place to catch musical performances.
Located in Chiado, the 1867 Teatro da Trindade INATEL is the place to go for theatre, film, opera, music, and ballet.
Teatro São Luiz, originally founded as Theatro Dona Amélia in 1894, offers theatre, music, dance, and talks.
Politeama Theatre, opened in 1913, is perhaps the most popular theatre in Lisbon. It hosts many Revista shows, musicals, and other popular performances.

Tram 28

Yes, it's very touristy. But it's also iconic. Tram 28 winds through some of Lisbon's oldest neighbourhoods – Graça, Alfama, and Baixa – giving you hilltop views, tiled buildings, and the occasional heart-racing turn. Go early to avoid the crowds and grab a window seat.

tram28lisbon.info

Surfing at Carcavelos Beach

Just a short train ride from Lisbon, Carcavelos – with a lively beach scene – is the perfect spot to try surfing. Rent a board or take a beginner's lesson; no-one will judge your wipeouts here.

carcavelossurfschool.com

Cycle or ride along the river Tagus

Rent a bike or electric scooter and cruise along the riverfront from Cais do Sodré to Belém. You'll pass museums, street art, cafés, and enough photo ops to fill your feed.

booking.lisbonbikerentals.com

Stand-Up Paddle Boarding in Cascais

Hop on a train to Cascais for calm waters and a stand-up paddle session. It's easier than surfing and much more peaceful. Plus, you might spot some fish or jellyfish (the friendly kind).

surfnpaddle.com

Hike or picnic at Monsanto Forest Park

Lisbon has its own massive 'secret forest'. Bring snacks and your playlist and explore. There are hiking trails, hidden viewpoints, and enough shade to hang out all afternoon. You can go to the park by bus. Or go by foot or bike and use the Corredor Verde de Monsanto, also known as the Green Corridor of Lisbon.

António Mega Ferreira Library

Lisbon's newest literary gem never closes its doors, making it a 24/7 haven for book lovers and night owls alike. This library honours António Mega Ferreira, the visionary behind Expo'98. It is sleek and modern, with cosy corners for late-night study sessions or quiet reflection.

Pavilhão de Portugal, Alameda dos Oceanos, Parque das Nações

Klaey Kreative – Pottery Painting

Need a break from sightseeing? Head to this super cute pottery painting studio where you can customise mugs, plates, or whatever your inner artist chooses. Perfect for rainy days.

Avenida Frei Miguel Contreiras 54 D, 1700-213 Alvalade, klaeykreative.com

↓ SANTA MARTA LIGHTHOUSE IN CASCAIS

FAMOUS PEOPLE

Amália Rodrigues

The voice of Portugal's most emotive music, Fado, known for songs about love, longing, and *saudade* (that untranslatable Portuguese feeling of beautiful sadness). Born in Lisbon, Amália became an international star but always remained rooted in her city. Today, her house is a museum. You will certainly hear her name and music all over Lisbon, especially in Alfama. If you're looking for music that hits deep, she's your introduction to Portugal's soulful side.

Michael Fassbender & Alicia Vikander

In search of a more relaxed lifestyle, away from the spotlight, Hollywood actors Michael Fassbender and Alicia Vikander bought property overlooking the River Tagus in 2019. Michael Fassbender, known from films like *X-Men*, *12 Years a Slave*, *Kneecap*, and *Black Bag*, was raised in Ireland. Alicia Vikander, known from films like *The Danish Girl*, *Tomb Raider*, and *Rumours*, was raised in Sweden. They met while filming *The Light Between Oceans* and now raise their own two children in Lisbon.

António Guterres

Not all famous Portuguese are singers or athletes. António Guterres, born in Lisbon, is the Secretary-General of the United Nations. He used to be Portugal's prime minister and now works on global peace, climate change, and humanitarian issues. He might not trend on TikTok, but he's shaping world policies and still shouts out Portugal when he can. Pretty impressive.

Cristiano Ronaldo

You can't talk about Portugal without bringing up CR7. Born on the island of Madeira, Cristiano Ronaldo is arguably the most famous Portuguese person on the planet. He's played for Manchester United, Real Madrid, Juventus, and now Al Nassr, but no matter where he goes, he plays for Portugal – hard. There's even a Ronaldo Museum in Madeira and a statue of him at the airport. Whether you're into football or not, you'll have seen his face on posters, perfume ads, and souvenir tops everywhere in the country.

Daniela Ruah

If you're into crime shows, you might recognise Daniela Ruah from *NCIS: Los Angeles*, in which she played tough agent Kensi Blye for over a decade. What many fans don't know is that she has deep Portuguese roots. Born in Boston but raised in Portugal from the age of five, Daniela started acting in Portuguese TV shows as a teen and quickly became a household name. She later made the leap to Hollywood but never left her roots – she directs and works on projects in both countries. Fluent in English and Portuguese, she's a great example of how you can blend cultures and thrive internationally while still showing love for where you come from.

João Félix

Another footballer making waves is João Félix. He grew up in Viseu and became a star at Benfica before moving to Atlético Madrid, Chelsea, and Barcelona. He's been called one of the most promising young talents in Europe. While Ronaldo is the legend, Félix is the future and very relatable to younger fans chasing their own dreams.

José Mourinho

Love him or hate him, José Mourinho can't be ignored. One of the most successful and confident football managers ever, he's from Setúbal, a coastal city just outside Lisbon. Mourinho has coached Chelsea, Real Madrid, Inter Milan, and Roma, but he never forgets his Portuguese roots.

Keanu Reeves

Here's a fun fact: Keanu Reeves' father has Portuguese heritage. While Keanu himself didn't grow up in Portugal, he's mentioned his background a few times, and Portuguese fans certainly claim him as one of their own.

Madonna

A few years ago, Madonna moved to Lisbon. No big deal. She bought a mansion in Sintra, enrolled her kids in local schools, and started sharing photos of sunsets and horses in the Portuguese countryside. Why? She said Portugal helped her slow down and get inspired again, especially by the local music scene. She's since moved out, but Lisbon definitely had its 'Madonna era', and locals still talk about it.

Nicole Kidman

In 2023, Nicole Kidman and Keith Urban quietly bought a riverside apartment in Parque das Nações, joining the growing list of stars choosing Lisbon as their luxurious second home.

Sara Sampaio

Born in Porto, former Victoria's Secret Angel Sara Sampaio is a supermodel representing Portuguese beauty on the global stage. She's modelled for major brands and acted in several films.

Scarlett Johansson

While she's super private, Scarlett Johansson is rumoured to have spent time in Lisbon, especially around Chiado and Príncipe Real. She reportedly owns a place in Portugal and has spoken in interviews about her love for quiet European cities that aren't mobbed by paparazzi. Lisbon checks all those boxes.

Shawn Mendes

Pop star Shawn Mendes may be Canadian born, but his father is Portuguese, and Mendes has talked about his summer holidays in Portugal and feeling connected to his roots. He's been spotted enjoying time in Lisbon, blending in like a local with his low-key vibe.

FILMS & SERIES IN AND ABOUT PORTUGAL

On Her Majesty's Secret Service (1969)

The sixth instalment of the James Bond series. Secret agent James Bond, played by George Lazenby, takes on SPECTRE's leader Ernst Blofeld, who plans to poison the world's population. Scenes were filmed in Hotel Estoril Palacio and on Guincho Beach in Cascais. Lisbon provides the backdrop to the reunion of Bond and Tracy.

The State of Things (1982)

German director Wim Wenders often chose Portugal as a setting for his films. In *The State of Things*, winner of the Golden Lion at the 1982 Venice Film Festival, a film crew is shooting a science fiction film in Lisbon. They run out of money and their producer mysteriously disappears. Filming took place in central Lisbon in the early 1980s, particularly around Cais do Sodré, capturing the bohemian spirit of the time. The Texas Bar, which was the setting for some of the most iconic scenes, has sadly disappeared over time.

The Russia House (1990)

John Le Carré's *The Russia House* is partly shot in Lisbon. Sean Connery plays British publisher Bartholomew Scott Blair, a heavy drinker whose life is turned upside down when he is recruited by British intelligence. Katya Orlova, a Russian publisher played by Michelle Pfeiffer, tries to find Blair to deliver a manuscript to him. She passes it on to a publisher's representative instead, who delivers it to the government. 'Barley' owns a holiday flat in central Lisbon.

The House of the Spirits (1993)

The House of the Spirits is an adaptation of Isabel Allende's novel, narrating the life of a Chilean family amidst a revolution that eventually culminates in the 1973 military coup. Although set in South America, many scenes were filmed in Lisbon. Among the film's notable settings is São Roque Church (see page 54). Actors include Meryl Streep, Jeremy Irons, Antonio Banderas, and Glenn Close. Both director Bille August and Jeremy Irons returned in 2013 to film *Night Train to Lisbon*.

Primal Fear (1996)

This classic courtroom thriller stars Richard Gere. But what's the Portuguese connection? In one bar scene, Gere's character hears a beautiful song and asks about it. The song is *Canção do Mar* by legendary Portuguese Fado singer Dulce Pontes. Off screen, Gere was so moved by her voice that he personally insisted the track be included in the film.

The Ninth Gate (1999)

Roman Polanski's *The Ninth Gate*, featuring a 34-year-old Johnny Depp, has become a cult classic. Whilst seeking the last two copies of a demon text, an antiquarian (Johnny Depp) gets drawn into a conspiracy with supernatural overtones. It was filmed in France, Portugal, and Spain in the summer of 1998. Portuguese scenes were shot at Biester Palace in Sintra, which serves as the mansion of reclusive book collector Victor Fargas.

Night Train to Lisbon (2013)

Based on the novel by Pascal Mercier, this film follows a Latin teacher (Jeremy Irons) who prevents a Portuguese woman from jumping off a bridge in Switzerland. The woman disappears, leaving behind a book by a Portuguese author and a train ticket to Lisbon. The teacher travels to Lisbon to uncover the author's past and the woman's identity. *Night Train to Lisbon* is filmed in Lisbon's beautiful old neighbourhoods and includes interesting questions about life and identity.

The Year of the Death of Ricardo Reis (2020)

Inspired by José Saramago's novel, this artsy, philosophical film is set in Lisbon during the 1930s. It's based on one of Fernando Pessoa's many alter egos and blends history, poetry, and surreal conversations with the dead.

Glória (2021)

This is Netflix' first series from Portugal. It is a spy thriller set in Portugal during the 1960s at a time when Portugal was still under a fascist dictatorship. At the height of the Cold War in the small village of Glória do Ribatejo, João Vidal embarks on espionage missions that could change the course of Portuguese and world history. Glória reveals key chapters in Portugal's history that remain little-known elsewhere. It is shot at different locations, including Lisbon.

Rabo de Peixe (Turn of the Tide, 2023)

This Netflix series takes place in the Azores, Portugal's remote island chain. It is a crime drama about a group of teens who find a massive stash of cocaine that washes up on shore. Think *Outer Banks*, but with stormy oceans, volcanoes, and Portuguese attitude.

Poor Things (2023)

Poor Things shows a fictionalised take of Lisbon, with trams flying and exaggerated colour contrasts. Protagonist Bella Baxter (played by Emma Stone) is discovering the world for the first time. In this version of Lisbon, she finds an explosion of sensations, with Carminho's Fado music, stunning landscapes, and the famous *pastéis de nata*. Bella devours sixty in a single scene!

BOOKS IN & ABOUT PORTUGAL

The Alchemist – Paulo Coelho

Not technically set in Lisbon, but this book is legendary in the Portuguese-speaking world. A young shepherd follows his dream across continents, learning lessons about love, destiny, and courage. It's short, dreamy, very relatable, and perfect for travellers chasing something they can't quite explain. Though it spans deserts and borders, the spirit of the story feels right at home in Portugal's tradition of exploration and soul-searching.

Alentejo Blue – Monica Ali

Set in a sleepy Portuguese village, this book weaves together the lives of locals and visitors trying to make sense of love, loss, and belonging. There's no big drama – just small, powerful moments that capture the heart of rural Portugal. If you liked *Normal People* by Sally Rooney, you'll love this.

The Book of Disquiet – Fernando Pessoa

This isn't a novel – more like the poetic diary of a deeply introspective man living in Lisbon a century ago. He overthinks, he observes, he writes things like 'to exist is to be missing', and somehow, it hits. This is a book for daydreamers, overthinkers, and anyone who wants to feel the quiet, moody side of Lisbon. Best read in a café with a *pastel de nata*.

Eyes Open – Lyn-Miller-Lachmann

Portugal, 1967. A teen gets caught between being a good student and speaking up against a brutal dictatorship. Written

in verse, this book is personal, powerful, and hits deep. It's short and poetic. Perfect if you want to get to know Portugal's past and root for someone standing up for what matters at a young age.

Forest Dancer – Susan Roebuck

A young ballet dancer from London escapes to rural Portugal to recover from injury and perhaps even from herself. Instead of fame and the spotlight, she finds a quiet village surrounded by forests, secrets, and people living by different rhythms. This one's for the dreamers, the artists, and anyone who's ever needed to hit pause on life. It is a book about healing, finding unexpected friends, and falling in love with a place that feels like the opposite of everything you thought you wanted. Peaceful, emotional, and very atmospheric.

The High Mountains of Portugal – Yann Martel

By the author of *Life of Pi*, this book is a surreal mix of road trip, grief, and magic realism – all set against the haunting backdrop of northern Portugal. Told in three linked stories, it mixes quirky humour with deep emotion. For the adventurous reader who doesn't mind weird (in a good way).

Night Train to Lisbon – Pascal Mercier

Imagine waking up one day, ditching your entire routine, and hopping on a train to Lisbon to chase down the story of a mysterious writer. That's exactly what a quiet Swiss teacher does – and he ends up wandering Lisbon's old streets, uncovering secrets, memories, and deep life questions. It is a thriller but also reads like a love letter to Lisbon itself.

Night Train to Lisbon – Emily Grayson

With the same title as the famous best-seller comes a different story. A woman uncovers a hidden past and jumps on a train to Lisbon to figure it all out. There's mystery, old-school romance, and secrets waiting in the city's shadowy corners. Perfect if you love a good mystery with a touch of vintage Europe.

The Villa of Dreams – Lucy Coleman

When a young woman heads to the Algarve to help restore a villa, she finds more than just sunshine – think family secrets, new friendships, and a fresh start under the Portuguese sun. A feel-good escape with beachy vibes, emotional twists, and a setting that'll make you want to stay forever.

FUN FACTS

Not just old ... ancient!

Think Paris and Rome are old? Lisbon's been around even longer – since around 1200 BCE. It's one of the oldest cities in the world and the second oldest capital in Europe. Athens takes the number one spot. Every alley has serious historical vibes.

Almost not the capital

Back in the 12th century, Coimbra in central Portugal was the country's capital. Lisbon only became the capital until 1255, mostly because it was easier to defend and had better sea access. Imagine a world where Lisbon was just a beachside city.

Portugal left its mark ... even in Japan

In the 1500s, the Portuguese were the first Europeans to make it all the way to Japan. And they didn't just trade goods, they also left behind words. Japanese still uses *pan* for bread (from *pão*) and *sabato* for Saturday (from *sábado*). Proof that Portuguese influence reached much further than most people think.

The oldest bookshop in the world

If you're into books (or just beautiful historic spaces), don't miss Bertrand Bookstore in the Chiado neighbourhood. It's been around since 1732, making it officially the oldest operating bookstore in the world. The outside is covered in pretty mosaics, and inside it's pure warmth and bookish magic. Perfect for getting lost in stories, both on the shelves and in the building itself.

The narrowest street

A street in Alfama called Travessa do Almada is just three feet wide – one of the narrowest in Europe. Two people can barely pass without doing a little side shuffle.

Golden Gate Bridge – But not

Lisbon has a bridge that looks just like the one in San Francisco ... but it's not. The 25 de Abril bridge might make you do a double take as it looks a lot like the Golden Gate Bridge. It was built by the same American company, but it's not an exact copy. It is longer, it sways like crazy, and it also carries trains. But don't call it the 'Portuguese Golden Gate' – locals will politely correct you.

Fado = Fate (and Feelings)

Fado isn't just music, it's pure emotion. Born on the backstreets of Lisbon (in Alfama), this emotional style started with everyday people singing about love, loss, and longing. Just one voice and a guitar, pouring out a feeling called *saudade* – a deep, beautiful kind of sadness you can't really explain. The word Fado literally means fate. It's raw, real, and straight from the heart of Lisbon.

Sardines: Lisbon's summer obsession

While Portugal is generally known for its seafood, Lisbon is absolutely obsessed with sardines, especially grilled. During the June street festivals, people queue for grilled sardines on bread. Heads, bones, skin – everything. You don't have to have it, but you will definitely be offered one, or more.

More sunshine than most of Europe

Lisbon gets around three hundred days of sun a year,

much more than London, Paris, and even parts of Italy. Bring sunglasses, not umbrellas. In summer, Lisbon gets up to nine hours of peak sun, and a UV index that can reach 10 or even 11, some of the highest in Europe.

Cork Capital of the World

Portugal has the largest cork forests on the planet and produces over 70 per cent of the world's cork. But it's not just for wine bottles – locals turn cork into everything from coasters to surprisingly stylish bags and accessories. Hit a street market and you'll find cork goods that are eco-friendly, lightweight, and totally gift-worthy.

Ravens

Lisbon's coat of arms contains a ship with a raven standing on each end. This is all connected to the city's patron saint, St Vincent of Saragossa. According to legend, ravens guarded his body from wild animals after his death, and some stories even claim that ravens piloted the ship that brought his remains to Lisbon centuries later. Until the last member of that flock died in 1978, ravens were housed in the cloisters of Sé de Lisboa. The raven remains a symbol of the city even now.

PHOTO SPOTS

Alfama

All of the Alfama neighbourhood is one big photo spot. The narrow streets, tiled walls, music wafting from the windows ... it's the Lisbon you came for. Get lost on purpose, snap the details (a door, a cat, a laundry line), and you'll end up with the most authentic shots of your trip. Stick around at sunset; when the light hits the rooftops, it's pure magic. No filter needed!

Miradouro Santa Luzia

Largo de Santa Luzia, 1100-487 Alfama

Located in the heart of Alfama, this viewpoint is perfect. With its tiled terrace, vine-draped columns, and a postcard-perfect view of red rooftops and the river, it's one of the most romantic spots in Lisbon. You'll often hear live Fado or soft guitar music in the background, adding to the dreamy, old-world vibe.

Chafariz da Rua do Arco a São Mamede

Rua do Arco a São Mamede 10, 1250-026 Santo António

This hidden gem near Príncipe Real is all about vintage Lisbon energy. The tiled fountain, arched passage, and soft light make it feel like you've stepped into an painting from another time. It's usually quiet, so you can get the shot without a crowd in the background.

Estufa Fria

*Parque Eduardo VII,
1070-051 Areeiro*

If you're into plants, this one's for you. Hidden inside Parque Eduardo VII, Estufa Fria is a lush greenhouse filled with ferns, waterfalls, and dreamy jungle energy. It is peaceful, photogenic, and kind of feels like you stepped into a fantasy novel, with quiet corners perfect for reading or journalling. Wander slowly, you might spot turtles sunbathing.

Palácio dos Marqueses de Fronteira

*Largo de São Domingos 1,
1300-472 Areeiro*

Tucked away from the usual tourist routes, Palácio Fronteira feels like a secret royal escape. The palace is filled with detailed *azulejos*, peaceful gardens, fountains, and staircases that look like they belong in a period drama. It's quiet, elegant, and a little surreal, like stepping into a dream scene from a historical fairytale. If you're into hidden gems with serious fairytale energy, this one's for you.

Pink Street

*Rua Nova do Carvalho 21,
1200-291 Cais do Sodré*

It's bold. It's loud. It's literally pink. Once a sketchy part of Cais do Sodré, now it is full of neon lights, bars, and umbrella art. Early morning gives you clean, crowd-free shots. At night? Think party energy, glowing signs, and chaotic fun. It's a classic Lisbon photo stop.

Elevador da Bica

*Rua da Bica de Duarte
Belo, 1200-054 Cais do
Sodré*

This steep, narrow street with its vintage yellow tram is one of Lisbon's most iconic photo spots. Stand at the bottom and shoot up for full dramatic effect.

LX Factory

Rua Rodrigues de Faria 103, 1300-501 Alcântara

Once an industrial zone, now one of Lisbon's coolest hangouts. LX Factory is packed with street art, quirky boutiques, awesome cafés, and artsy corners. The vibe is edgy but welcoming – think weekend markets, rooftop bars, and spots like Ler Devagar, a bookshop with flying bikes and stacked shelves. It's the kind of place where you come for a cup of coffee and end up staying for hours.

MAAT – Museu de Arte Arquitetura e Tecnologia

Avenida Brasília 1300-598 Belém

This museum looks like a spaceship landed on the riverbank. The curves of the white tiled building and the reflections at sunset create a magical picture. You can walk on the roof for wide angle shots of the river and bridge. It's futuristic, minimal, and completely different from Lisbon's usual old-town aesthetic.

Jardim do Rio

Rua do Alvito, 1200-157 Almada

This riverfront park is relaxed, local, and full of little moments you'll want to capture – like the 25 de Abril Bridge stretching into the sunset, picnic scenes, and dogs living their best lives. It's a perfect spot to slow down, have a snack with friends, or just people watch while the golden light hits the water.

FOOD AND DRINKS

BREAKFAST, BRUNCH & COFFEE

Dear Breakfast

This is a brunch lover's heaven, with runny eggs, fluffy pancakes, great coffee, and soft lighting everywhere. Each location offers a unique setting, blending modern design with classic Portuguese charm. Whether you're nestled in the historic streets of Alfama or enjoying the vibrant atmosphere of Chiado, Dear Breakfast provides a delightful start to your day.

dearbreakfast.com

Augusto Lisboa

A charming café known for its vibrant décor and delicious brunch options. With plenty of vegan and vegetarian options, it's a favourite for relaxed mornings and casual meetups.

Rua de Santa Marinha 26, 1100-491 Alfama, augusto-lisboa.res-menu.com

Café da Garagem

Hidden inside a theatre, Café da Garagem has insane views over Lisbon, especially at sunset. The café is moody, artsy, and feels like a secret even locals forget about. Grab a drink, gaze out the giant windows, and let your main character moment happen.

Costa do Castelo 75, 1100-178 Graça, teatrodagaragem.com

Do Beco Santos

Do Beco serves sourdough, good vibes, and house made everything. With a laid-back, plant-filled vibe across two locations, it's perfect for a relaxed breakfast or a calm work session. Don't miss the cinnamon rolls — they sell out fast.

Rua Passsos Manuel 106, 1150-260 Arroios; Rua São João da Mata 18, 1200-849 Estrela; paodobeco.com

Esplanada Café

This open-air café is made to chill out. Grab a table under the trees, order a *bica* or a freshly squeezed juice, and soak up the laid-back Príncipe Real energy. It's the kind of place where time slows down and no one's in any rush to leave. You'll find their kiosks on Campo de Santa Clara and Avenida da Liberdade.

Praça do Príncipe Real, 1250-184 Príncipe Real, insta @esplanadaprincipereal

Marquise da Mobler

A bakery, concept store, and coffee shop all in one, with a serene garden at the back that's perfect for catching up with a friend for hours. Enjoy handcrafted coffee whilst browsing unique items, from Portuguese ceramics to vintage furniture and handwoven textiles from Mexico and Peru. Pro tip: don't leave without trying a *pão de deus*, a delicious coconut-topped pastry that's basically made to go with coffee. And if you're into furniture, check out Mobler nextdoor while you're at it!

Rua Nova de Piedade 33, 1200-296 Misericórdia, insta @marquisedamobler

Seagull Method

Right in the heart of Lisbon, Seagull Method is the go-to spot for brunch lovers. This aesthetic café offers SO many brunch options ... from the classic French toast, waffles and pancakes to more adventurous dishes like monkfish, polenta, and *syrniki*. It's one of those places that makes you want to come back just to try everything on the menu.

Rua Da Palmeira 23, 1200-311 Misericórdia, insta @seagullmethodcafe

Comoba

This is your spot if you are into clean eating. A minimalist dream café with plenty of plant-based options, all beautifully plated, and very photogenic. Think matcha, mushroom lattes, and natural light that makes your avocado toast look like a piece of art. Bonus: Wi-Fi and laid-back work vibes.

Rua Da Boavista 90, 1200-085 Misericórdia, comoba-lisboa.com

Hello, Kristof

Small, stylish, and effortlessly cool. This café is all about good coffee, clean design, and quiet focus. The shelves are stacked with indie mags, the flat whites are on point, and the vibe is ideal for solo hangs, slow mornings, or journalling with zero pressure.

Rua do Poço dos Negros 103, 1200-337 Misericórdia, hellokristof.com

Cafe Janis

Indoor-outdoor, super social, and full of energy. It's got Paris café flair with Lisbon sunshine. Go for brunch or cocktails — either way, the outdoor space is prime for people watching and casual hangs.

Rua Moeda 1A, 1200-109 Misericórdia, insta @cafejanis

Curva

A relaxed neighbourhood café tucked into Graça's hills, with a menu full of comfort food and great vegetarian options. Relaxed atmosphere, friendly staff, and a small back garden make this one feel like a local secret.

Rua Damasceno Monteiro 108D, 1170-113 Misericórdia, insta @curvalisboa

UAIPI Bebida e comida Brasileira

Colourful, bold, and packed with Brazilian flavour. From açaí bowls to cheesy *pão de queijo* and refreshing drinks, UAIPI is where you go when you want tropical energy and a break from the typical brunch menu. Super friendly, super fun.

Travessa Isabéis 18, 1200-761 Estrela, insta @uaipi.mandioca

Neighbourhood

A corner café with natural wines, good coffee, and effortless style. It's half local hangout, half creative studio energy, for quiet afternoons that somehow turn into wine evenings with new friends.

Largo Conde-Barão 25, 1200-163 Estrela, neighbourhoodlisbon.com

Heim Café

A minimalist café serving hearty brunches and specialty coffees. With its cosy interior and welcoming vibe, it's a go to spot for both locals and visitors.

Rua de Santos-o-Velho 2 e 4, 1200-812 Santos, insta @heimcafe.lisbon

Cafetaria Picasso

An old-school Portuguese café with timeless charm. Come for strong coffee, toasties, and that local feel where you're more likely to hear real conversations than see laptops.

Rua Barata Salgueiro 31, 1250-141 Alvalade

PASTÉIS DE NATA

Manteigaria

Famous for buttery pastry and those iconic burn marks on top, Manteigaria is beloved by locals and travellers alike. Open-style counters let you see the magic happen. Grab a warm *pastel* dusted with cinnamon and walk it off down Rua Augusta.

manteigaria.com

Fábrica da Nata

Trendy, modern, and fully *nata* focused. Fábrica serves up warm tarts alongside coffees and light snacks in a bright, stylish space. It's a great place to sit, have a snack, and rest your legs.

Rua Augusta 275A, 1100-052 Baixa; Praça dos Restauradores 62-68, 1250-110 Restauradores, fabricadanata.pt

Casa São Miguel

A little spot tucked into the hills of Alfama. Their *natas* are rustic, rich, and feel homemade, in the best way. Ideal for a pitstop while getting lost in the local area.

Rua De Sao Miguel 5, 1100-542 Alfama, casasaomiguel.pt

Pastéis de Belém

This is the one that started it all, having baked the custard tarts to their secret recipe since 1837. The crust is crisp and golden, the custard is warm, and yes, it's touristy, but 100% worth queuing for. The queue can be long, but placing your order online will save you quite some time.

Rua De Belém 84 92, 1300-085 Belém, pasteisdebelem.pt

GELATO

Santini

A Lisbon gelato legend. Known for its rich flavours and super creamy textures, Santini is a must-visit. There are several locations, but the one in Chiado is especially popular – a vibrant spot offering classic and seasonal flavours.

Rua do Carmo 9, 1200-093 Chiado, santini.pt

Mu Gelato

A contemporary gelato shop owned by Italians from Verona. Traditional meets experimental, offering a range of innovative as well as traditional flavours.

Rua da Escola Politécnica 20, 1250-096 Príncipe Real, mugelato.pt

Nannarella

Probably Lisbon's most beloved gelato spot. Creamy,

rich, and Italian-approved. There is always a queue, but it moves fast, and their gelato is 100% worth the wait.

Rua das Janelas Verdes 96, 1200-692 Santos, nannarella.pt

FOOD COURTS

Time Out Market

Lisbon's most famous food hall. Big names, long tables, and a buzzing crowd. Ideal if you want to try everything at once – just be ready for a wait. Pro tip: go mid-afternoon to avoid the lunch rush.

Mercado da Ribeira, Avenida 24 de Julho, 1200-479 Cais do Sodré, timeoutmarket.com

Mercado Campo Ourique

A laid-back, local alternative to the Time Out Market. Smaller, more relaxed, and packed with everything from burgers and sushi to Portuguese *petiscos*.

Rua Coelho da Rocha 104, 1350-075 Campo de Ourique, insta @mercadodocampoourique

Mirari

A lush, open-air lounge with seriously good vibes. Picture palm trees, soft lighting, and a DJ spinning into the night. It's part cocktail bar, part secret garden – perfect for evening hangs, date nights, or just vibing under the Lisbon sky.

Avenida 24 de Julho 170, 1350-352 Estrela, mirari.pt

8 Marvila

A hidden gem in Lisbon's coolest up-and-coming neighbourhood, 8 Marvila is an industrial style food court that brings top-notch food, craft drinks, shops, and plenty of creative energy. Whether you're after gourmet burgers, sushi rolls, or vegan bowls, this place has it all. The vibe is urban, artsy and very Marvila: young, fun, and full of weekend energy.

Praça David Leandro da Silva 8, 1700-007 Marvila, 8marvila.com

LUNCH & DINNER

Cantina das Freiras

A 'secret' canteen run by nuns with one of Lisbon's best river views. Affordable, simple meals under €10, and a rooftop that feels like your own hideaway. Arrive early — it's tiny and fills up fast.

Travessa Ferragial 1, 1200-184 Baixa, insta @cantinadasfreiras

Panda Cantina

Tiny space, big ramen. Locals rave it's 'the best honest ramen in town'. Expect a minimal menu, fast service, and low-key atmosphere. A rare gem in touristy Baixa.

Rua Da Prata 252, 1100-052 Baixa, insta @pandacantina

Lisboa tu e eu

Tucked away on a quiet corner of Alfama, this spot feels like stumbling on someone's secret kitchen. With a simple, welcoming vibe and classic, homemade dishes and locals humming along to the music. Perfect for a slow lunch after getting lost in the neighbourhood.

Rua De Adiça 58, 1100-116 Alfama, insta @lisboatueeualfama

O Velho Eurico

A must for foodie explorers. This *tasca* upgrades Portuguese classics — think octopus *lagareiro*, piglet *empanada*, and more. Cosy but popular, so get there early.

Largo de São Cristóvão 3, 1100-179 Alfama, insta @ovelhoeurico

Taberna Sal Grosso

No-frills tavern serving traditional Portuguese dishes with a modern twist. Expect hearty portions, friendly vibes, and a seasonal menu.

Calçada do Forte 22, 1100-256 Alfama, insta @tabernasalgrossoalfama

Páteo 13

You can't visit Lisbon without diving into its food scene, and Páteo 13 is unforgettable, with fresh fish and juicy cuts of meat straight off the charcoal grill. Try sardines with boiled potatoes and grilled peppers; and don't skip the sangria! No indoor seating, just a lively outdoor crowd. Only open in warmer months.

Calçadinha de Santo Estêvão 13, 1100-502 Alfama, insta @pateo13

Lautasco

Tucked away in a charming courtyard, Lautasco serves traditional Portuguese food in a vibrant setting. A hidden gem, perfect for a relaxed meal away from the crowds.

Beco do Azinhal 7, 1100-067 Alfama, lautasco.eatbu.com

Tasca Pete

A fun *tasca* where traditional Portuguese comfort food gets a modern twist. Think small plates, natural wine, a great staff, and an industrial yet homey atmosphere.

Rua Angelina Vidal 24A, 1170-113 Graça, insta @tasca.pete

Zé da Mouraria

Big flavours and a Lisbon legend. Famous for giant portions of traditional food — especially the cod dishes are renowned. Loud, packed, and very local. Arrive hungry.

Rua Joao do Outeiro 24, 1100-292 Mouraria, insta @ze_da_mouraria

Zero Zero

Naples comes to Lisbon with perfect woodfired pizzas. The garden seating at the Príncipe Real location is perfect for sunny lunches or wind-down dinners. The whole place has that easy going, always-full energy. With four locations across the city, it's a go-to for locals who take their pizza (and tiramisu) seriously.

pizzeriazerozero.pt

Magnolia

A cosy all-day spot in one of Lisbon's prettiest squares. Magnolia serves everything from Turkish eggs and fresh smoothies to natural wines and small plates. Great for brunch, even better for golden hour. Sit outside, watch the world go by, and don't be surprised if you find yourself staying longer than planned.

Praça das Flores 43, 1200-192 Príncipe Real, insta @magnolia_lisboa

Empanar

Empanar is a laid-back *empanada* place in Lisbon's artsy neighbourhood Bica, right by the iconic yellow tram. They serve Argentinian style *empanadas* (with vegan options), delicious cocktails, and sweet treats. It's perfect for a casual snack, quick coffee, or a low-key dinner hangout.

Rua da Bica de Duarte Belo 44, 1200-259 Misericórdia linktr.ee/empanar.pt

La Malquerida

This is the perfect spot to grab some delicious tacos. The best part? Show up between 6 and 7pm any day of the week, and the tacos are just €1 each! They even offer gluten-free tacos and quesadillas, so there's something for everyone. Malquerida's €1 taco hour draws a crowd, so don't be surprised if you need to queue. But this spot lives up to the hype.

Travessa Do Marquês de Sampaio 14, 1200-262 Misericórdia, insta @tacoslamalquerida

El Santo Lisboa

Mexican street food meets rooftop party vibes. Think tacos, tequila, and neon signs. Come for a casual bite and stay for the cocktails and DJ sets on weekends.

Pátio do Tijolo 61, 1250-095 Misericórdia, insta @el.santo.lisboa

Boavista Social Club

Right in the heart of Cais do Sodré, Boavista Social Club mixes laid-back dining with a great atmosphere. It starts as a casual spot for dinner – serving creative, Mediterranean-style small plates and natural wines – and slowly transforms into a lively hangout with DJs and a fun crowd. The space has that perfect in-between vibe: relaxed but buzzing, stylish but not trying too hard. Whether you're going for the food, the music, or just the energy, it's one of those places that makes you feel like you're in the right place at the right time.

Rua da Boavista 16, 1200-275 Cais do Sodré, insta @boavista.socialclub

Mano a Mano

Stylish Italian with a cool crowd and a pasta menu worth committing to. Inside, it's moody and modern; outside, it's great for dinner with friends or a pre-night-out bite.

Rua Do Alecrim 22, 1200-014 Cais do Sodré, insta @eatatmano

Insaciável

A laid-back wine bar offering a curated selection of natural wines and small plates. Perfect for catching up with friends over good food and even better drinks.

Rua da Esperança 156, 1200-808 Santos, insaciavel.pt

Da Noi

Tucked in Madragoa's narrow streets in Estrela, Da Noi feels more like a dinner party than a restaurant. It's small, atmospheric, and run by people who clearly love what they do. Their menu is seasonal and Mediterranean-inspired; they serve handmade pasta, fresh local veggies, and natural wines that makes you want to slow down and enjoy every sip. The vibe is relaxed but stylish, perfect for a night out with friends or a quiet, romantic dinner. It's the kind of hidden gem you'll tell your favourite people about.

Rua do Machadinho 44, 1200-707 Estrela, insta @danoi.lisboa

Taqueria Paloma

A vibrant taqueria bringing Mexican street food to Lisbon's trendy Marvila district. Flavourful tacos, refreshing cocktails, and a lively atmosphere.

Praça David Leandro da Silva 9A, 1950-064 Marvila, taqueriapaloma.com

Ponto Final

Right by the river with unbeatable sunset views of Lisbon. You'll take a ferry, walk along the water, and arrive at this classic spot with its signature yellow tables. Order fresh fish and *vinho verde* and stay till golden hour hits. Booking is a must.

Rua Do Ginjal 72, 2800-285 Almada, insta @pontofinalrest

Atira-te ao Rio

Just a few steps from Ponto Final, this spot is a bit more low-key, but the location is just as magical. Rustic, by the river, and perfect for a long lunch. Atira-te ao Rio means 'throw yourself into the river' but the food keeps you at the table.

Rua Do Ginjal 69, 2800-285 Almada, insta @atirateaorio

BRING THE PARENTS

Cervejaria Ramiro

Old-school seafood spot that's packed every night. Order garlic shrimp, clams, crab, and buttered toast and don't forget the *prego* (steak sandwich) at the end. Casual vibes, serious flavour.

Avenida Almeida Reis 1H, 1150-007 Arroios, cervejariaramiro.com

Rocco

Fancy, flashy, and totally vibey. Italian classics served in a glam setting with velvet booths and golden light. Perfect for dressing up and indulging your 'I'm living abroad' fantasy – even if it's just for a night.

Rua Ivens 14, 1200-227 Santo António, rocco.pt

A Cevicheria

Chef Kiko's iconic Peruvian fusion spot. The giant octopus sculpture on the ceiling sets the tone, and the *ceviche* is next level. Creative, fresh, and ideal for a dinner that will impress your parents as well as you.

Rua Dom Pedro V 129, 1250-096 Príncipe Real, acevicheria.pt

Rosamar

A laid-back yet stylish seafood grill and oyster bar in Lisbon's trendy Príncipe Real neighbourhood. Designed by Studio Pim, the interior has seaside vibes with nautical touches. It's the perfect spot to bring your parents. It's stylish enough to feel cool, but relaxed enough to keep things casual, and the vibe makes Rosamar a guaranteed crowd pleaser.

Rua da Rosa 317, 1200-381 Príncipe Real, restaurantrosamar.com

Canalha

A stylish spot, blending Portuguese classics with contemporary flair. Chef João Rodrigues crafts dishes that are both innovative and comforting, earning Canalha a nod by Bib Gourmand.

Rua da Junqueira 207, 1300-338 Belém, canalha.pt

↓ BIKE BAKERY, INSTA @BIKE_BAKERY

FADO

Fado is Lisbon's most famous music style — emotional songs about love, longing, and life, usually performed with a Portuguese guitar. In many Fado restaurants, songs are performed between courses. The lights are dimmed; it's a beautiful, soulful moment — remember to pause your conversation and soak up the moment!

Tasca do Chico

One of the most famous Fado bars in Lisbon and still one of the most atmospheric. It's tiny and packed, but when the music starts, the place goes quiet. You'll find a mix of locals, travellers, and the occasional teary-eyed tourist. No-frills, full of soul.

Rua dos Remédios 83, 1200-109 Alfama, tascadochico.com

A Baiuca

A true Alfama classic where the Fado singers perform right at your table. A Baiuca feels less like a restaurant and more like someone's kitchen during a family celebration. It's intimate, raw, and incredibly local. Expect shared tables, spontaneous singing, and a lot of heart.

*Rua São Miguel 20, 1100-544 Alfama, insta @abaiuca_*

Mesa de Frades

Set in a 18th century former chapel, this place is pure Fado meets drama. Candlelight, *azulejos*, and top-class performers make it one of the most atmospheric spots in town. Book ahead: Mesa de Frades is popular.

Rua dos Remédios 139, 1100 Alfama, mesadefrades.pt

Clube de Fado

This is one of the more polished and upscale Fado venues, but it is still authentic. Clube de Fado combines elegance with emotional intensity. Go there if you want to hear the greats perform over dinner in a setting that's classy but never stiff.

Rua São Jorge da Praça 86-94, 1100-521 Alfama, clubedefado.pt

Tasca do Jaime

Casual and totally unfiltered. This is the kind of place where the show starts in the middle of the afternoon, the regulars know every single word, and your drink is more likely to come in a plastic cup than a wine glass. Less curated, more real. Go for the experience.

Rua da Graça 91, 1170-165 Graça, insta @tascadojaime

Cante de Poeta

An intimate Fado house just across the river in Alcântara, Cante de Poeta feels like stepping into a heartfelt performance rather than a venue. Home to passionate performances and a curated set menu, this spot is one of Lisbon's best-kept secrets. There's something extremely beautiful about the way the guitar strings echo off the stone walls, wrapping around you like a familiar story. If you want to feel Fado beyond the tourist façades, this is where the city's soul comes out to sing.

Calçada do Livramento 4–6, 1350-115 Alcântara, cantodopoeta.com

WINE

Esplanada da Graça

This one's for sunset chasers and daydreamers. Esplanada da Graça sits high up in Lisbon's hills and has one of the best panoramic views in the city — no filter needed. Located in the scenic Graça neighbourhood, it's shaded by pine trees and filled with mismatched chairs and locals lounging with a beer. Grab a cold drink, maybe some olives or a toastie, and slow

down. Early evening, it turns into a low-key hangout with soft background music and groups of friends sharing bottles of *vinho verde*. If you're lucky, you'll catch someone strumming a guitar. This place feels like the calm after the storm — in the best possible way.

Largo da Graça, 1100-114 Graça, insta @esplanada_da_graca

Vino Vero

Natural wine bar with the cool factor. Tucked into a little corner of Graça, this is where you sip funky orange wines and snack on delicious small plates. It's golden hour magic when Vino Vero catches the evening light, and the vibe is intimate but social.

Travessa Do Monte 30, 1170-265 Graça, vinovero.wine

Secret Garden LX

Hard to find, even harder to leave. Secret Garden LX is a hidden sanctuary nestled

between São Bento and Estrela. This lush hideout feels more like a backyard jungle than a bar. It's the kind of place where you sip a mojito, lose track of time, and before you know it, it's midnight.

Beco Carrasco 1, 1200-096 Graça, insta @secretgarden_lx

Black Sheep

A wine bar for people who don't take wine too seriously, with local bottles and relaxed vibes. It's a perfect spot for relaxed people-watching with a glass of local red or *pét-nat* in hand.

Praça das Flores 62, 1200-192 Príncipe Real, blacksheeplisboa.com

Quiosque da Ribeira das Naus

A riverside kiosk with lounge chairs, breezy vibes, and drinks that go down easy. Perfect for sunset beers, Aperol spritzes or just watching boats drift by. Scenic and very 'wish you were here'. Perfect for pre-dinner drinks or a slow afternoon where nothing needs to happen.

Avenida da Ribeira das Naus 5, 1200-000 Cais do Sodré, insta @ribeiradasnausquiosque

Cave da Estrela

Tucked away near the beautiful Estrela Basilica, Cave da Estrela is a haven for natural wine lovers. It specialises in low-intervention, Portuguese-only wines and is great for a nice tasting session in the evening. It's the kind of place where strangers become friends over a shared bottle, and each sip comes with a story of sun-soaked vineyards and old-world winemaking. Think relaxed vibes, friendly staff, and discovering new wines you never knew existed.

Travessa de São Plácido 48B, 1200-806 Estrela, insta @cavedaestrela

Holy Wine

A tiny wine bar with a major soul. Holy Wine is a hidden treasure for natural wine lovers. Specialising in natural and small-batch wines, it's the kind of place where you chat with the owner, try something new and end up staying longer than planned. They often have a good playlist too.

Calçada de Estrela 15, 1200-661 Estrela, insta @holywinelisbon

COCKTAILS

Lost In

Colourful outdoor seating with boho cushions and panoramic views. Great for a relaxed lunch, dreamy cocktails, or a break from the city buzz. It's giving world-traveller energy — without ever leaving Lisbon.

R. Dom Pedro V 56D, 1250-094 Príncipe Real, lostinrestaurante.com

Foxtrot

A retro-style bar with speakeasy vibes. Think dimmed lights, vintage sofas, and classic cocktails. It's perfect for smaller groups, quiet convos, or a romantic date night that calls for something moody and nostalgic. The hidden courtyard at the back is a secret worth discovering, especially on warm nights.

Travessa da Galé 1, 1200-161 Príncipe Real, barfoxtrot.pt

Palivlhão Chinês

Find the red door, ring the bell and step into Pavilhão Chinês, a hidden gem in Bairro Alto. A grocery store from 1901, now a very interesting bar packed with vintage toys, art, and random collectibles — it's like stepping into a funky museum, but way more fun. Grab a cocktail, wander through five rooms of weird and wonderful treasures, and challenge your friends to a game of pool.

Rua Dom Pedro V 89, 1250-093 Príncipe Real, barpavilhaochines.blogspot.com

Park Bar

Rooftop bar on top of a parking garage – literally. It's a hidden oasis with panoramic views, chilled cocktails, and a laid-back crowd that leans creative and effortlessly cool. Perfect for starting the night with a drink above the city.

Calçada do Combro 58, 1200-115 Bairro Alto, insta @parklisboa

Secret Poets Society

Step through a secret door near the Carmo Convent into a moody, Pessoa-inspired speakeasy. At Secret Poets Society, vintage typewriters, candlelight, and Pessoa quotes on the walls set the tone. The crowd is stylish and quiet, the bartenders are part artist, part alchemist. Come for a midweek moment of magic, but don't forget to book in advance.
Open Wednesday-Saturday evenings. Make a reservation.

Travessa do Carmo (exact location revealed at booking), Cais do Sodré
insta @the_secret_poets_society

Fábrica Braço de Prata

What used to be an old weapons factory is now one of the best creative spaces in the city. Located in Marvila, Fábrica Braço de Prata is part gallery, part concert venue, part café, part bookshop – basically, a cultural playground. You can watch live jazz, catch a film screening, stroll through an art show, or just hang out with a drink and see what unfolds. It's raw, unexpected, and packed with local art and energy. No two nights are ever the same.

Rua da Fábrica de Material de Guerra 1, 1950-128 Marvila, bracodeprata.com

The Kissaten

Tucked away just off Avenida da Liberdade, The Kissaten is like a secret retreat for music and whisky lovers. Inspired by Japanese listening bars, this spot is all about dimmed lights, vinyl records, and seriously smooth vibes. You can flip through their curated record collection, put some music on, and sip from Lisbon's biggest selection of whisky – they stock over a hundred kinds. It's a nice hangout for when you want good sound, good drinks, and zero chaos.

Rua de Santa Marta 61, 1150-294 Avenida da Liberdade, insta @thekissaten

The Red Frog

Hidden behind an unassuming red door, The Red Frog speakeasy transports guests to the Prohibition era with its vintage décor and clandestine vibe. Once inside, you'll discover a world of expertly crafted cocktails, dimmed lighting, and jazz tunes that set the mood. Booking is recommended, as this hidden gem is popular among those in the know. It's the perfect spot for an intimate date night or a sophisticated evening with friends.

Rua do Salitre 5A, 1250-004 Avenida da Liberdade, redfrog.pt

CLUBS

Bairro Alto

This area is Lisbon's classic kick-off spot. Narrow streets packed with tiny bars, cheap drinks, and music spilling into the alleys. Bar hop, make new friends, and go into the night with zero plans.

Tribe Social Club

Right in the heart of Chiado, Tribe Social Club is where work meets play without the boring in between. By day, it's a relaxed coworking spot where you can grab a coffee, plug in your laptop, and get stuff done. By night, it flips into a social hangout with cocktails, music, and events that draw a creative, international crowd. Whether you're freelancing, people-watching, or just in it for the vibes, Tribe is the kind of place that makes productivity feel cool.

Praça Luís de Camões 22, 1200-243 Chiado, tribesocial.co

Pensão Amor

One of Lisbon's most unique spots, located in the vibrant Cais do Sodré area. Once a brothel in the city's red-light district, now an awesome bar. This place has a lot of character with its old-school charm, eccentric décor, and fun surprises. Their themed rooms are filled with everything from vintage erotica to hidden corners, and from a burlesque-style lounge to a stylish library. Have a creative cocktail, catch live performances, and keep your eyes peeled — famous faces like to hang out there too. You never know who you might bump into!

Rua do Alecrim 19, 1200-292 Cais do Sodré, pensaoamor.com

MusicBox Lisboa

An underground club — literally and in spirit — located under the arches of Cais do Sodré. At MusicBox, Lisbon's alternative scene thrives. It is known for indie bands, electro sets, and alternative parties. Gritty, loud, and loved by the local crowd.

Rua Nova do Carvalho 24, 1200-019 Cais do Sodré, musicboxlisboa.com

Lisbon Rio

Right by the river, this club has indoor as well as outdoor dance spaces, Latin and hip-hop nights, and a crowd that is dressed to impress. This feels like a summer party that never ends.

Cais Gás 14, 1200-109 Cais do Sodré, lisboario.pt

Rua Cor-de-Rosa (Pink Street)

Lisbon's famous party strip. Bright pink pavements, neon signs, packed bars, and a vibrant energy throughout the night. Rua Cor-de-Rosa is super touristy but also super fun. Go there for chaos and late-night stories.

Rua Nova do Carvalho 21, 1200-019 Cais do Sodré

Bicaense

A low-key bar with a neighbourhood feel, neon lights, and underground vibes. Known for its art exhibitions, indie DJ sets, and after-dinner drinks that turn into dancing. A local favourite that likes to keep things casual. Expect a little weird, a lot of fun, and no pressure to impress.

Rua de São Paulo 83, 1200-413 Cais do Sodré, insta @bicaense_est.1959

Monsantos Open Air

A forest party inside Lisbon; a literal rave in the woods. This is a huge outdoor venue in Monsanto Park with live music, DJ sets, and a mini festival vibe. It's the perfect summer escape when you want music, movement, and moonlight all in one. Check their schedule as it is event-based.

Estrada da Circunvalação 1400-061, Benfica and Belém, monsantosopenair.pt

Lux Frágil

Lisbon's most legendary club. Multi-level, riverfront, and packed with dancers and creatives. With big name DJs and a seriously late-night crowd. The rooftop offers a breath of fresh air and unbeatable views of the River Tejo, while the music downstairs stays loud and hypnotic. Don't show up too early, as things start late.

Avenida Infante Henrique, Sta Apolónia Cais da Pedra 1950-376 Santa Apolónia, luxfragil.com

Casa Independente

Part bar, part cultural space, part cool kid hangout. Set in an old mansion with mismatched furniture, live music, and a tiger print room. Weird, artsy, and totally Lisbon. Check their calendar; there is always something different going on.

Largo do Intendente Pina Manique 45, 1100-285 Intendente, casaindependente.com

QUEER

Finalmente Club

Small, loud, and full of character, Finalmente is a legendary drag and dance club that stood the test of time. There's no velvet rope or dress code, just good energy, loud music, and a crowd that's ready to celebrate anything.

Rua da Almada 117, 1100-016 Baixa, finalmenteclub.com

Trumps

Lisbon's most iconic LGBTQ+ club, opened in the 80s and still going strong. Expect drag shows, themed parties, and a packed dance floor that doesn't quit till sunrise. Welcoming, wild, and full of energy. Whether you're queer, curious, or just ready to celebrate life, a good time at Trumps is guaranteed.

Rua da Alegria 120, 1250-007 Príncipe Real, trumps.pt

HOW TO DRESS LIKE A LOCAL

The Portuguese style is hard to define, but you'll know it when you see it.
Lisbon locals somehow pull off outfits that scream 'I just threw this on' – even though every piece is clearly doing something on purpose.

The vibe? Confidence and chaos. Especially talking about the Portuguese *girlie*, who the internet officially fell in love with last year. Think Vicky Montanari and Caetana and other fashion muses mixing florals with stripes, trainers with pearls, and somehow making grandma sweaters feel like luxury. No rules, just vibes.

For the guys, it's all about looking like you didn't try, while clearly trying. A well-worn jacket, good trainers, a slightly oversized tee, and the permanent energy of 'I'm going to a DJ set as well as the market'.

Flip-flops are a no, unless you're actually walking on sand. Not to forget Lisbon's hills, which will judge you for wearing them. But don't forget: sunglasses are mandatory, even in the shade. Scarves aren't just for warmth, they're for drama. And if your outfit isn't at least a little confusing, are you even Lisbon-coded?

In short: wear whatever you want but make it look intentional, even if it's just linen and vibes.

FLEA MARKETS

Feira da Ladra

Campo de Santa Clara, 1100-472 Alfama, insta @feira_da_ladra_lisbon

Lisbon's oldest and most iconic flea market has been around since the 13th century and still provides the ultimate treasure hunt. Open Tuesdays and Saturdays, it spreads across Campo de Santa Clara, with everything from vintage vinyl and army jackets to handmade jewellery, dusty books, and total randomness. Bargaining is part of the ritual, and early birds catch the best finds. Feira da Ladra is chaotic, charming, and a Lisbon rite of passage if you love second-hand adventures.

Mercado de Santa Clara

Campo de Santa Clara, 1100-472 Alfama

Right next to Feira da Ladra, this covered market is a quieter gem. On market days, it offers shelter from the Lisbon sun, and during the week it's home to local food vendors, arts and crafts, and rotating exhibitions. It's also a great pitstop if you're browsing the flea market and need a place to grab a snack, use a real toilet, or just sit down and people-watch without missing any of the action.

Anjos70 Art & Flea Market

Praça David Leandro da Silva 8, 1700-007 Marvila, anjos70.org

Anjos70 is the creative heart of Lisbon's alternative market scene. Held monthly (mostly on weekends), it brings local designers, vintage collectors, illustrators, and foodies under one roof. You'll find funky second-hand clothes, handmade ceramics, and vegan treats, often with a live DJ or acoustic set thrown in the mix. It's the kind of place where you show up for a tote bag and leave with earrings and a screen print. Although Marvila is its main location, the Art & Flea Market sometimes pops up at a different site. Check their website before you go.

VINTAGE & SECOND-HAND

Flamingos Vintage Kilo Lisboa

Rua da Conceição 48, 1100-150 Baixa, flamingoslisboa.com

Flamingos Vintage Kilo Lisboa is fun, loud, and full of colour-coded racks. It's great for oversized jackets, denim, and throwback streetwear. You pay by weight, so light items mean big wins.

A Outra Face da Lua

Rua da Assunção 22, 1100-044 Baixa, aoutrafacedalua.com

A little bit retro, a little bit rock-and-roll. A Outra Face da Lua has a serious personality. You'll find racks of 80s and 90s fashion, quirky pins, and accessories that feel plucked straight out of a cool basement. Their playlist is always good, their prices are fair, and in the café in the back you can sip a cappuccino surrounded by weird and wonderful clothes.

Ás Espadas

Calçada do Carmo 42, 1200-091 Chiado, insta @as.de.espadas

A clean, curated space with vintage pieces that are more refined than random. At Ás Espadas, it's about quality fabrics, sharp tailoring, and finding that one jacket or blazer that just works.

Joker Vintage Store

Calçada do Carmo 26/28, 1200-091 Chiado

Right next to Ás Espadas, Joker goes a little louder – bright prints, old-school band tees, and one-of-a-kind accessories. The vibe is playful, nostalgic, and a little punk. It's a great spot for mixing statement pieces with your everyday look.

LX Popup

Rua Maria 66A, 1170-210 Arroios, insta @popup.lx

Located in the creative heart of Anjos, LX Popup is a rotating concept store that brings together fashion, design, and art with a conscious twist. It's the kind of place where you might find limited edition trainers one week and handmade ceramics the next. The vibe is relaxed and community-driven, attracting a mix of local artists, designers, and curious shoppers. If you're into discovering unique pieces and supporting sustainable brands, this spot is worth a visit.

Retro City Lisboa

Rua Maria Andrade 43, 1170-216 Arroios, insta @retrocitylisboaArroios, insta @popup.lx

This shop is big, colourful, and packed with personality. From Hawaiian shirts to leather jackets to 70s glassware, Retro City feels like walking through your coolest aunt's attic. It's perfect for statement pieces and spontaneous try-ons.

Retrox Vintage Shop

Rua dos Anjos 4C, 1150-038 Arroios

Small but mighty, this local shop is known for well-priced basics and vintage staples. Think denim, printed shirts, and timeless outerwear that doesn't scream costume. A great place to build a unique outfit without blowing your budget.

Humana Vintage

Avenida Almirante Reis 26B, 1150-018 Arroios, humana-portugal.org

A go-to for thrifters on a mission. Humana is a charity shop chain with super affordable prices, especially during their rotating sales (sometimes everything is priced at just €2!). It's hit-or-miss, but when it hits, it hits hard.
Vinyl and vintage, all under one roof. Tropical

VINTAGE & SECOND-HAND

Tropical Bairro – Vintage & Record Shop

Rua do Forno do Tijolo 1, 1170-132 Arroios, insta @tropicalbairro

Bairro brings together vinyl lovers and vintage chasers in one space. The clothes are good, the records are well curated, and the atmosphere is mellow and filled with music. It has the perfect Sunday vibe.

Amor Fati

Rua de Rosa 158, 1200-381 Misericórdia, insta @amor.fati.lisbon

Moody, artsy, and a little bit mysterious. Think layered neutrals, candles, ceramics, and independent fashion labels that feel more art than trend.

POP Closet

Rua Horta Seca 24, 1200-221 Misericórdia, insta @popclosetofficial

With an eye for quality, POP Closet leans into pre-loved designer items, luxe fabrics, and timeless cuts. If your style is minimalist but expensive, this is your place. The shop is sleek, calm, and totally confidence-boosting.

Madame Surtô

Rua de São Bento 111, 1200-815 Estrela, madamesurto.pt

Step inside for instant vintage overload in all the best ways. Madame Surtô mixes second-hand clothes, quirky decor, and rotating art shows in a space that feels more like an eccentric friend's apartment than a shop.

Loja Baú

Rua de S o Bento 202, 1250-219 Estrela, lojabau.com

Half antique store, half cabinet of curiosities, Loja Baú is for treasure hunters with a soft spot for the weird and wonderful. You'll find vintage homeware, old postcards, retro toys, and random gems that make no sense but are just great.

Dear Vains

Rua Rodrigues de Faria 103, 1300-501 Alcântara, insta @dearvains

This spot is underground, both literally and aesthetically. Dear Vains sits inside LX Factory and serves up moody, alternative fashion with a vintage twist. Great for finding something unexpected or just absorbing the cool kid energy.

STREETWEAR

Cybercafe Skateshop

Ferragial 1, 1200-182 Baixa, cybercafeskateshop.com

A no-frills spot with serious skate cred. Boards, wheels, shoes, and loose-fit tees with zero pretension. True sakers come here.

Nude Project

Rua Áurea 153, 1100-060 Baixa

A vibe-packed boutique blending minimalist aesthetics with bold streetwear. Expect clean, high-quality basics - think sleek tees, comfy hoodies, and statement outerwear - that effortlessly mix comfort with edge.

Son of a Sun

Rua da Assunção 107, 1100-043 Baixa, sonofagun.eu

Made in Portugal, made for the sun. This brand's all about effortless coastal vibes, linen shirts, breezy fits, and clean aesthetics. Perfect for beach days or just looking like you've had one.

Latte Lisbon

Rua Nova do Almada 61, 1200-288 Chiado, lattelisbon.com

Minimalist, clean, and full of carefully selected pieces, Latte Lisbon is all about slow fashion with a modern edge. If you're into timeless silhouettes and neutral tones, this is your spot. Think basics that are anything but basic.

The Feeting Room

Calçada do Sacramento 26, 1200-394 Chiado, thefeetingroom.com

Part concept store, part sneaker heaven. The Feeting Room in Chiado brings together cool local brands, edgy streetwear, and minimalist design in one stylish space. You'll find everything from standout sneakers to carefully curated clothing and accessories. Bonus: there's a cozy café inside, perfect for a break between browsing.

Breed – Urban Concept Store

Rua Nova do Almada 47, 1200-288 Chiado, breedlisboa.com

Streetwear lives here. Breed stocks edgy, hard-to-find brands with a big focus on trainers and standout pieces. Come for the fits; stay for the mood.

Santo Loco

Rua da Rosa 206, 1200-391, Bairro Alto, santoloco.com

A skate shop made fashion. Santo Loco carries a curated range of skate brands with a big dose of style. Boards, sneakers, hoodies ... you know the drill.

Slumdog Lisbon

Rua da Atalaia 24, 1200-041 Bairro Alto, slumdoglisbon.com

Part gallery, part streetwear label, all attitude. Slumdog is for anyone who wants to wear art and not follow rules.

Original Project

Rua de São Paulo 172, 1200-429 Cais do Sodré, insta @originalproject

Bold and graphic-heavy, this Lisbon born label is all about storytelling through streetwear. It feels local, but globally aware.

Ericeira Surf & Skate

Centro Colombo, Avenida Lusíada, 1500-392 Carnide, ericeirasurfskate.com

A big-name favourite for surf lovers. Whether you're into skating or just want comfy, laid-back clothes, this place delivers.

FASHION & DEPARTMENT STORES

Amar Lisboa

Rua do Carmo 87, 1200-093 Baixa,
insta @amar_lisboa

This shop is like Lisbon in T-shirt form. Amar Lisboa showcases colourful graphic designs made by local artists: bold prints, statement totes, and playful souvenirs you'll actually want to keep yourself. It's artsy, affordable, and full of Lisbon personality.

Armazéns do Chiado

Rua do Carmo 2,
1200-093 Chiado,
armazensdochiado.com

Located in a historic building once destroyed by fire and brought back to life, Armazéns do Chiado is Lisbon's closest thing to a classic department store. Inside, you'll find a mix of well-known international brands, beauty counters, and fashion retailers, plus a food court with views over the town. It's convenient, centrally located, and perfect for a quick retail fix between sightseeing.

Bernardo Atelier

Rua Dom Pedro V 74, 1250-094 Príncipe Real,
insta @b.atelierlisboa

This modern atelier is where clean cuts meet personal touch. Bernardo, a Lisbon-based designer, creates elevated staples with minimalist silhouettes and structured tailoring. The space feels part showroom, part creative lab, and you might even catch the designer at work. If you're into fashion that's thoughtful, wearable, and made locally, this is a must-visit.

LX Factory

Rua Rodrigues de Faria 103, 1300-501 Alcântara, lxfactory.com

LX Factory is a former factory turned cultural playground. A maze of unique boutiques, vintage shops, great cafés, and rooftop bars. There's street art everywhere and there's always something happening, making it a favourite hangout for locals and visitors who want to soak up Lisbon's creative vibe.

8 Marvila

Praça David Leandro da Silva 8, 1950-143 Marvila, 8marvila.com

Once a massive wine warehouse, 8 Marvila is now a buzzing creative spot where you'll find art galleries, indie shops, and little cafés all tucked into an industrial setting. It's the perfect place to wander, explore, and discover something new around every corner.

BOOKSHOPS

Livraria Bertrand

Rua Garrett 73-75, 1200-203 Chiado, bertrand.pt

The world's oldest bookshop still feels fresh, blending centuries of history with the excitement of new releases. Wander from room to room, each with its own charm, and you'll feel like you're part of a story that's still being written.

Books of Wonder

Rua da Misericórdia 103, 1200-275 Chiado booksofwonder.pt

Don't let the name fool you, this is not the New York store. The one in Chiado focuses on art books, illustrated editions, and literary events.

Tigre de Papel

Rua de Arroios 25, 1150-053 Arroios, tigrepapel.pt

Tigre de Papel is both a bookshop and a cultural space. They focus on the local community with workshops, debates, and readings in a welcoming, creative atmosphere. Their stock is a mix of bargain books, zines, and plenty of local titles that capture Lisbon's indie spirit.

Good Company Book Store

Avenida Visconde De Valmor 2, 1000-291 Avenidas Novas, goodcompanybookstore.com

A bright spot that's equal parts bookshop and café. It's also the perfect place to meet up with a friend for coffee and conversation or just curl up with a good read on a rainy Lisbon afternoon.

Poesia Incompleta

Rua de São Ciro 26, 1200-831 Príncipe Real, insta @ livraria.poesia.incompleta

A tiny haven for poetry lovers, this bookshop is dedicated to verse – old, new, rare, and even custom-ordered. Whether you're into modern voices or classic Portuguese poets, the vibe here is all about quiet magic. It feels like a secret corner of Lisbon that only poetry lovers get to know.

Livraria da Travessa

Rua da Escola Politécnica 46, 1250-102 Príncipe Real, travessa.pt

Brazilian in roots, Portuguese in spirit. Livraria da Travessa mixes Portuguese and international literature in a welcoming space. From poetry to art books, this spot feels like a living room for Lisbon's creative scene.

Letra Livre

Calçada do Combro 139, 1200-113, Bairro Alto, letralivre.pt

This is a place for true literature lovers: no flashy displays, just shelves full of carefully chosen books in literature, poetry, and the humanities. Grab a book, sit by the window, and let the city's energy fade into the background.

Ler Devagar

Rua Rodrigues Faria 103, 1300-501 Alcântara, livrariadatravessa.com.br

Inside LX Factory this iconic bookshop has it all: art books, fiction, a café, and even a flying bicycle suspended from the ceiling. Ler Devagar is where Lisbon's creativity comes to life.

Snob – Livraria e Editora

Travessa de Santa Quitéria 32A, 1250-220 Campo de Ourique, livrariasnob.pt

Part bookshop, part publisher. Snob's shelves are stacked with small press gems, philosophical reads, poetry, and alternative voices that push boundaries. They also host events and launch parties that give this place a vibrant pulse.

Livraria Cultura

Avenida da Liberdade 231, 1250-142 Avenida da Liberdade, livrariacultura.pt

Spacious, modern, and full of variety. Livraria Cultura is perfect for those days when you just want to wander. It's a place to recharge, with a small café to fuel your browsing, and a community vibe that brings Lisbon's literary crowd together.

Linha de Sombra

Rua Barata Salgueiro 39, 1250-059 Avenida da Liberdade, linhadesombra.com

Hidden away inside Lisbon's film archive, Linha de Sombra is a cultural treasure chest. The shop focuses on art, cinema, photography, and poetry, making it perfect for anyone who's a little bit of a dreamer.

Photo Book Corner

Rua Marquês Sá da Bandeira 86C, 1050-150 Picoas, photobookcorner.com

This place is a love letter to photography. Its focus on photo books and artist editions means that every visit feels like a fresh window into a new visual world. The clean, curated space makes it easy to get lost in the images — and if you're even a little bit visually oriented, it's impossible to leave without something that sparks your imagination.

Salted Books

Calçada Marquês de Abrantes 96, 1200-720 Santos, saltedbooks.com

Salted Books is a lovely little English-language bookshop in the Santos neighbourhood that feels like a home away from home. It isn't just a shop, it's a community hub, with regular events like author talks and writing workshops that make you want to come back again and again.

ART SUPPLIES

Mão Livre

*Rua da Prata 256-258,
1200-120 Baixa,
maolivre.com*

In the heart of Baixa, Mão Livre is a haven for illustration and creative prints. Expect hand-drawn pieces, artist collabs, and quirky postcards that turn everyday notes into mini works of art. It's a bright, cheerful spot that reflects Lisbon's vibrant creative scene.

A Vida Portuguesa

*Largo do Intendente Pina Manique 23 1100-285 Arroios,
avidaportuguesa.com*

Part store, part time capsule, A Vida Portuguesa celebrates Portugal's design heritage. From soaps and ceramics to vintage-inspired stationery, it's a nostalgic journey through the best of Portuguese craftsmanship. A Vida Portuguesa has three locations, with its flagship store in trendy Arroios.

Amarelo28

*Rua de São Miguel 70,
1100-535 Alfama,
insta @amarelo28_gifts*

Tucked away in Alfama, Amarelo28 is an indie design studio and shop that's full of surprises. From minimalist posters to bold prints, it's a place where graphic design meets Lisbon's colourful spirit.

Papelaria Fernandes

*Largo do Rato 13,
1250-186 Rato,
papelariafernandes.com.pt*

An icon in Lisbon since 1891, Papelaria Fernandes is where old-school stationery meets modern design. From gorgeous notebooks to fine writing tools, this place has everything you'll need to brighten up your desk (or journal). It's the kind of shop that makes you want to start sending postcards again.

TRIUNFAM SEMPRE
LICOR BEIRÃO
EXPOSIÇAO PORTUGUESA EM SEVILHA
SALUS
LICOR BEIRÃO

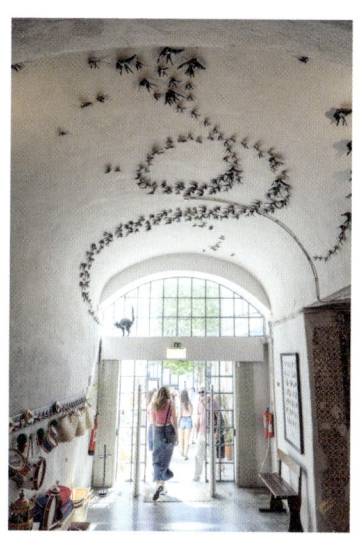

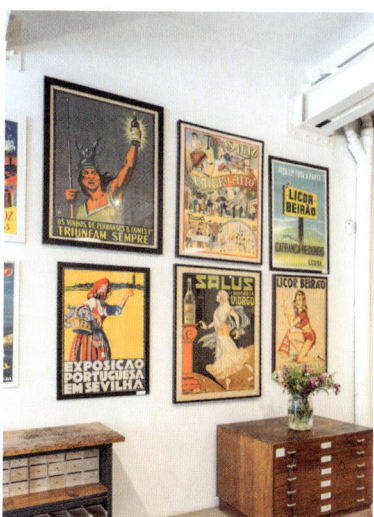

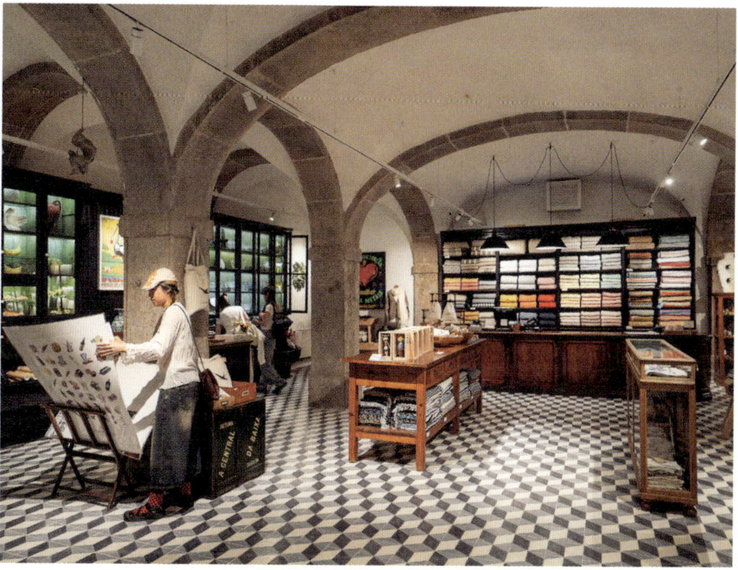
A CENTRAL
DA BAIXA

AFFORDABLE ART & HOME DECO

Paris em Lisboa

Rua Garrett 77, 1200-273 Baixa, parisemlisboa.pt

An institution in Lisbon, Paris em Lisboa has been around since 1888. Its refined selection of linens, tableware, and gifts is a nod to European elegance, with that timeless Lisbon touch.

Uma Cantik

Rua Tomás da Anunciação 43A, 1350-322 Baixa, umacantik.com

A splash of Bali in Lisbon. Think carefully curated home décor – cushions, ceramics, and textiles that feel equal parts Portuguese and Indonesian. The result? A shop that's effortlessly calm and full of natural beauty.

Cerâmica na Linha

Rua Capelo 16, 1200-224 Chiado, ceramicasnalinha.pt

A quiet studio and shop dedicated to ceramics. Everything is small-batch and handmade, from their earthy mugs to their delicate plates. Perfect if you're after something both beautiful and unique.

Pink Dolphin

Rua Poiais de São Bento 50, 1200-348 Príncipe Real, pinkdolphinlisbon.com

This fun, slightly retro boutique is all about statement pieces. From neon vases to playful prints, Pink Dolphin turns every corner into a conversation starter. It's the kind of place you pop into 'just to browse' and leave with your new favourite find.

Area Store

Avenida Eng. Duarte Pacheco, Torre 1, 8th floor, 1070-101 Areeiro, areastore.com

A Lisbon design landmark, Area Store blends global influences with a modern aesthetic. From minimalist furniture to quirky home accessories, this bright and spacious shop is where Lisbon's design lovers go to be inspired.

AFFORDABLE ART & HOME DECO

VINYL & CDs

Louie Louie

Escadinhos do Santo Espírito da Pedreira 100A, Baixa, louielouie.biz

Tucked into a charming Baixa corner, Louie Louie is a haven for music lovers. From jazz to indie to global grooves, the selection here is as warm as the friendly staff. It's the kind of place where you can lose track of time flipping through the records and chatting about everything from local bands to rare finds.

Tabatô Records

Rua de Arroios 100, 1000-042 Arroios, insta @tabatorecords

This shop leans into Lisbon's global roots with a fantastic selection of African, Brazilian, and Lusophone vinyl. It's small but packed with treasures, perfect for those looking for a deep cut or something with a fresh beat.

Amor Records

Rua Frei Francisco Foreiro 2A, 1150-166 Arroios, insta @records.amor

A fun shop with a warm vibe, Amor Records specialises in dance music – from house to disco, and everything in between. If you're ready to find the soundtrack to your next party, this is the spot.

Discoleção

Calçada Duque 53, 1100 Misericórdia

Part shop, part shrine to vinyl culture, Discoleção has been a Lisbon favourite for decades. Their carefully curated bins cover everything from Portuguese classics to global hits. It's a nostalgic, no-fuss spot that music nerds and casual fans alike find irresistable.

Mau Génio

Estrada de Benfica 731A, 1500-089 Benfica, maugenio.com

Part record shop, part cultural hub, Mau Génio is always alive. Their racks are a mix of fresh releases and vintage gems. They also host events that keep the local scene lively.

SHOPS WE LOVE

Cantê

Calçada Nova de São Francisco 10, 1200-300 Baixa, cantelisboa.com

This Lisbon-based swimwear brand nails that effortless beach style with their flattering cuts and playful prints. A must for sunny days and surf vibes.

Claus Porto

Rua dos Três Irmãos 8, 1200-890 Baixa, clausporto.com

A Lisbon classic since 1887, Claus Porto crafts bold, fragrant soaps and lotions in packaging that's almost too pretty to open. Step inside and you'll be hit with scents that feel like a little luxury escape.

Conserveira de Lisboa

Rua dos Bacalhoeiros 34, 1100-071 Baixa, conserveiradelisboa.pt

This old-school sardine shop with wooden cabinets filled from top to bottom with colourful tins became a style icon. Grab some of their retro tins for the ultimate Lisbon souvenir.

Benamôr

Rua dos Bacalhoeiros 22, 1100-070 Chiado, benamor1925.com

Born in Lisbon in 1925, this beauty brand has timeless charm with a Portuguese twist. The products, made with natural ingredients, come in dreamy Art Deco packaging. 100% local and the perfect spot to buy a gift.

Luvaria Ulisses

Rua do Carmo 87A, 1200-093 Chiado, luvariaulisses.co

A tiny Chiado shop that's been making gloves since 1925. Classic elegance in every stitch, complemented by the interior that hasn't changed since the shop first opened.

Embaixada

Praça do Príncipe Real 26, 1250-184 Príncipe Real, embaixadalx.pt

Inside a 19th century neo-Moorish palace, you'll find one of Lisbon's coolest concept stores. Slow fashion meets old-world glam. A rotating lineup of Portuguese designers, sustainable fashion labels, local artisans, and lifestyle brands is spread across vaulted rooms with chandeliers and tiled floors and there even is a courtyard bar for an après-shopping drink.

Loja Real

Praça do Príncipe Real 19, 1250-100 Príncipe Real, loja-real.com

Just across from Embaixada, Loja Real is a curated gem that champions everything Portuguese-made. From handcrafted ceramics to fashion accessories, everything feels intentional, quality-driven, and full of craftsmanship. This is your go-to for timeless pieces.

Solar Antiques

Rua Dom Pedro V 70, 1250-094 Príncipe Real, solar.com.pt

This shop is full of old, special tiles, beautiful furniture and rare ceramics. It's a great place to browse Portugal's history!

Latitid

Praça do Príncipe Real 26, 1250-184 Príncipe Real, latitid.com

Locally designed and globally admired, Latitid's swimwear combines sleek lines and laid-back energy, just like Lisbon itself.

Lost In

Rua Dom Pedro V 58, 1250-096 Príncipe Real, lostinindia.pt

Downstairs from the popular rooftop bar, this shop is a haven for boho-chic finds. From flowy dresses and comfy knits to unique home goods, it's full of laid-back Lisbon vibes.

PARKS AND SWIMMING

Miradouro Santa Luzia

Located above Alfama, this spot is like a balcony over the city. It's covered in flowers and has colourful tiles telling stories from Lisbon's past. From here, you can see the red rooftops and the sparkling river below. It's the perfect place to relax and soak up the sun. On weekends, musicians often play gentle songs that make you feel like you're starring in a film!

Largo de Santa Luzia, 1100-487 Alfama

Miradouro da Graça

This viewpoint is a little higher up and gives you a panoramic view of Lisbon. It's surrounded by shady trees, perfect for cooling down on hot days. You can even spot the Castelo de São Jorge from here! Bring a snack and find a spot on the benches or grab a drink from the small café nearby. In the evening, the golden light makes the whole city glow. It's a magical place for taking photos or just hanging out with friends.

Largo da Graça, 1170-165 Graça

Parque Eduardo VII

One of the biggest parks in Lisbon, Parque Eduardo VII is like a green river flowing downhill. Its carefully trimmed hedges create striking patterns, and you can climb to the top for an amazing view of the Tagus. The fresh breeze and big lawns make it a perfect spot for a picnic. If you're feeling active, it's also a great place to ride your skateboard or fly a kite!

Parque Eduardo VII, 1070-051 Avenidas Novas

Jardim do Torel

Imagine a hidden garden on top of a hill. That's Jardim do Torel. It's a small park with amazing views of Lisbon's rooftops and river. In summer, there's a special natural swimming pool — a shallow basin filled with cool water where you can splash and relax. The pool is only open for a short time each year, so check ahead! It's the perfect spot to escape the heat and hang out with friends.

Rua Júlio de Andrade, 1150-206 Santo António

Jardim do Príncipe Real

Jardim do Príncipe Real is a leafy park in the heart of one of Lisbon's most stylish neighbourhoods. This 19th century garden is known for its massive cedar tree, which creates a shady hideout that's perfect for reading or catching up with friends. On weekends, the park comes alive with a local market where you'll find everything from fresh veggies to crafts.

Praça do Príncipe Real, Príncipe Real

Jardim da Estrela

This park is filled with huge trees that offer plenty of shade — perfect for a summer day. It's opposite the beautiful Basilica da Estrela, so you can easily explore both. There's a small duck pond and even a little café in the middle of the park. You can stretch out on the grass and read a book or stroll along the winding paths. It's also a fun place to bring a frisbee or your favourite snacks for an outdoor feast.

Praça da Estrela 12, 1200-694 Estrela

Parque Florestal de Monsanto

If you're up for an adventure, head to Parque Florestal de Monsanto — Lisbon's biggest green space and the perfect spot for a nature escape. Covering over 1,000 hectares, this massive forest park is like the city's very own wilderness. You'll find winding hiking and biking trails, scenic picnic spots, and even some epic viewpoints from where you can see all the way to the river. Bring

your bike, your best playlist, and your favourite snacks for a day out in the fresh air!

Estrada da Bela Vista 1500-554, Lisbon

Jardim do Rio

Take a short ferry ride from Lisbon to Almada, and you'll find Jardim do Rio – a beautiful riverside garden. Walk along the water and watch the boats sail by. There are benches to sit on and green grass for picnicking. On sunny days, dip your toes in the river or explore the nearby waterfront cafés. Don't forget your camera, the views of Lisbon across the river are just incredible.

Rua do Ginjal 2800-285 Almada

VEGETARIAN AND VEGAN LISBON

Manjerica

Manjerica is a lovely little shop and café right by Praça da Figueira, the heart of downtown Lisbon. It's the perfect spot to grab a smoothie bowl, fresh juice, or even a hearty vegan wrap if you're on the go. Inside, you'll find shelves filled with organic products and local goods, making it a great spot to restock your pantry with vegan essentials.

Rua João das Regras, Praça da Figueira 5A, 1100-293 Baixa, manjerica.pt

Jardim das Cerejas

If you're a fan of buffets, Jardim das Cerejas is your dream come true! This vegetarian and vegan buffet is packed with colourful salads, hot dishes, and sweet treats. The all-you-can-eat style means you can try a bit of everything – perfect for indecisive eaters. And with a central location near Rua do Carmo, it's an easy stop while exploring downtown.

Rua do Carmo 87, 1200-093 Baixa, jardimdascerejas.com

Ao 26 – Vegan Food Project

One of Lisbon's best loved vegan restaurants, Ao 26 is always buzzing. The menu is fully plant-based, from mouthwatering vegan burgers to creative daily specials. Save room for dessert: their raw cakes are out of this world! It's a must-visit if you're around Chiado and craving some vegan comfort food.

Rua Vitor Cordon 26, 1200-484 Chiado, ao26.com

Organi Chiado

Just steps away from the bustling Chiado streets, Organi Chiado is a calm, peaceful restaurant serving organic vegetarian and vegan meals. Their dishes are light and refreshing, with lots of seasonal veggies and local ingredients. It's the perfect spot for a healthy lunch break!

Calçada Nova de São Francisco 2, 1200-300 Chiado, organi.pt

The Food Temple

Hidden in the maze of Mouraria's cobbled streets, The Food Temple is a magical vegan mecca. Their menu changes daily and is full of creative, global flavours such as Indian curries, Asian stir-fries, and Mediterranean plates. With its relaxed atmosphere and communal seating, it's the perfect place to meet new friends and share delicious food.

Beco do Jasmim 18, 1100-289 Mouraria, thefoodtemple.com

PSI

Tucked away in a lush garden near Arroios, PSI has been a vegetarian staple for years. With its fountain, leafy trees, and colourful plates, it's a dreamy place to slow down and enjoy a delicious vegetarian meal. The outdoor seating makes it feel like a secret garden; definitely worth checking out on a sunny day!

Alameda Santo António dos Capuchos, 1150-314 Arroios, psivegetariano.com

My Mother's Daughters

This cute spot is all about sustainability and slow living. My Mother's Daughters is a small café serving nourishing vegan meals, fresh juices, and delicious desserts. It's a great place for a quiet lunch or a sweet treat in a laid-back atmosphere.

Largo de São Sebastião da Pedreira 49, 1050-010 Avenidas Novas, mymothersdaughters.pt

Gaya Veggie Market

Don't forget to check out Gaya Veggie Market! This little vegan shop is stocked with everything from organic snacks to cruelty-free beauty products. It's a must-visit if you're looking to fill your kitchen (or backpack!) with tasty, ethical goodies.

Rua da Palmeira 15, 1200-311 Príncipe Real, gayaveggiemarket.pt

Eight – The Health Lounge

This health-focused café is a fun spot in the middle of the bustling Bairro Alto. It's all about vibrant plant-based plates, fresh juices, and smooth lattes. If you're on the hunt for a work spot, Eight's comfy couches and fast Wi-Fi make it a great choice.

Rua do Loreto 61, 1200-241 Bairro Alto eightlisbon.com

Vegan Junkies

For those times when only comfort food will do, Vegan Junkies has you covered. This lively spot dishes out plant-based burgers, loaded fries, and vegan chicken-style wings – the perfect fuel for a night out in Cais do Sodré!

Rua de São Paulo 234, 1200-435 Cais do Sodré, veganjunkies.pt

Kong – Legumi Sushi

Who said sushi is just for fish lovers? Kong's Legumi Sushi proves that plant-based sushi can be just as fresh and exciting. Their creative vegan rolls and bowls are full of colour and flavour, making them a hit with sushi fans and newbies alike.

Rua da Boavista 58, 1200-066 Cais do Sodré, legumisushi.pt

O Botanista

With its jungle-inspired interior and green dishes, O Botanista is a feast for the senses. Their menu has a bit of everything – brunch, lunch, and sweet treats. Plus, they have a shop section selling natural and eco-friendly goods, so you can stock up on

essentials while you're there.

Rua Dom Luís I 19, 1200-149 Cais do Sodré
obotanista.com

The Green Affair

Modern, chic, and 100% vegan. The Green Affair is great for a sit-down meal with friends. Their menu is varied and exciting, with everything from creamy pasta dishes to colourful poke bowls. Don't miss their vegan cheesecake for dessert!

Rua do Alecrim 12, 1200-014 Cais do Sodré
thegreenaffair.pt

OUTSIDE OF LISBON

Cascais

Cascais is a classic coastal escape. Golden beaches, cute cafés, and a breezy promenade make it ideal for sunbathing or surfing. Grab a gelato from a local shop, explore the small museums or take a break in the shady Marechal Carmona Park. If you're feeling adventurous, rent a bike and cycle along the coast to Guincho Beach, a wild stretch of sand known for its rugged beauty and spectacular sunsets. The train ride from Cais do Sodré is only 40 minutes, so you can wake up in Lisbon and be on the sand by lunchtime. Whether you're here for the surf, the shops, or just the salty breeze, Cascais has that perfect summer vibe all year round.

Comporta

Lisbon's answer to endless summer. Known for its wide, sandy beaches and chilled-out vibe, time slows down in Comporta. The beaches feel wild and untouched, with soft dunes and warm Atlantic breezes – perfect for long naps or barefoot walks. The little town is all about boho-chic charm, with stylish beach bars serving cold drinks and local dishes. Even though it's a bit of a drive (about 1.5 hours by car), the journey is part of the adventure — passing through pine forests and rice paddies that feel like another world. Once you're there, you'll see why Comporta is a favourite for many.

Costa da Caparica & Sesimbra

Costa da Caparica is Lisbon's go-to beach for lazy days in the sun. Stretching for miles, it has beach bars playing music, volleyball courts for casual games, and waves perfect for learning to surf. Bring a picnic or grab a bite at one of the funky beach bars — there's always something happening. Just around the corner, Sesimbra offers a totally different vibe. This sweet fishing village is famous for its fresh seafood and calm blue waters, and the cliffs above the beach are perfect for short hikes with epic views. Both spots are super easy to reach — just 30-45 minutes by bus or car from Lisbon.

Ericeira

Ericeira is a surfer's paradise with a laid-back atmosphere and epic Atlantic waves. Even if you're not surfing, it's a wonderful spot for beach walks, delicious seafood, and watching the waves roll in. It's about an hour by car, making it perfect for an easy day trip to the ocean.

Óbidos

Óbidos is like stepping back in time. The town is small enough to explore in a few hours, but there's so much to see. Stroll the cobbled streets, snap pics of the whitewashed houses, and sip sweet cherry *ginjinha* from edible chocolate cups. Art galleries, bookshops, and ancient churches hide around every corner, making it a place to get lost and found again. It's about an hour by car or bus from Lisbon – far enough for it to feel like an adventure, but close enough for a perfect day out.

Portinho da Arrábida & Galapinhos Beach

Just an hour from Lisbon, this stretch of coastline feels like the Caribbean – clear turquoise water, lush cliffs, and a total escape. Galapinhos beach is a must, but the whole area, known as Portinho da Arrábida, has several stunning beaches to explore. Bring a book and a towel, and don't rush. For lunch, hit the local restaurant O Farol – a calm spot with fresh seafood and unreal ocean views.

Sintra

Sintra is straight out of a fairytale. Picture colourful palaces, misty forests, and hidden gardens – it's no wonder this town is a UNESCO World Heritage Site! Its must-sees are the bright and quirky Palácio da Pena and the mysterious Quinta da Regaleira, with its secret tunnels and lush gardens. With a super easy 40-minute train ride from downtown Lisbon, Sintra is the perfect quick getaway for a day of exploration.

INDEX

Neighbourhoods 8
Practical info 12
Travel 14
Where to stay 20
Good to know 24
When to travel 30
Life in Lisbon 40
History 42
Sightseeing 50 (see below)
Museums & Galleries 58 (see below)
Street art 68
Cinema 72
Festivals 74
Things to do 78
Famous people 82
Films & series in and about Portugal 86
Books in & about Portugal 90
Fun Facts 96
Photo Spots 100 (see below)
Food and Drinks 106 (see below)
Going Out 128 (see below)
Shopping 142 (see below)
Green Lisbon 172
Parks and swimming 174
Vegetarian and vegan Lisbon 179 (see below)
Outside of Lisbon 184 (see below)

SIGHTSEEING 50
Arco de Rua Augusta 51
Castelo de São Jorge 51
Cristo Rei 55
Igreja de São Roque 54
Miradouros 50
Mosteiro de Jerónimos 55
Palácio da Ajuda 54
Panteão Nacional 54
Praça do Comércio 50
Sé de Lisboa 51
Torre de Belém 55

MUSEUMS & GALLERIES 58
B-MAD Bernardo Museum of Art Deco 61
Berardo Collection Museum 64
Calouste Gulbenkian Museum – Modern Collection 59
Calouste Gulbenkian Museum 59
Carmo Archeological Centre 58
Fado Museum 58
Galeria Zé dos Bois (ZDB) 60
Lisbon Story Centre 58
MAAT 64
MAC/CCB 64
MACAM 61
MUDE 58
Museu de Medeiros e Alemeida 60
Museu dos Coches 64
Museu Nacional do Azulejo 58
Museum of Design and Fashion 58
National Museum of Ancient Art 60
National Museum of Natural History and Science 60
Pavilhão do Conhecimento 61
Quake 64
Underdogs Gallery 61

PHOTO SPOTS 100
Alfama 100
Chafariz da Rua do Arco a São Mamede 100
Elevador da Bica 103
Estufa Fria 103
Jardim do Rio 104
LX Factory 104
MAAT 104
Miradouro Santa Luzia 100
Palácio dos Marqueses de Fronteira 103
Pink Street 103

FOOD AND DRINKS 106
8 Marvila 114
Atira-te ao Rio 124

Augusto Lisboa 108
Boavista Social Club 122
Breakfast, brunch & coffee 108
Bring the parents 124
Café de Garagem 108
Café Janis 110
Cafetaria Picasso 112
Canalha 126
Cantina das Freiras 116
Casa São Miguel 113
Cervejaria Ramiro 124
Comoba 109
Curva 110
Da Noi 123
Dear Breakfast 108
Do Beco Santos 108
Empanar 121
Esplanada Café 109
Fábrica da Nata 112
Food Courts 114
Gelato 113
Heim Café 112
Hello, Kristof 110
Insaviácvel 123
Lautasco 119
Lisboa tu e eu 116
Lunch & Dinner 116
Magnolia 121
Malquerida, La 121
Mano a Mano 122
Manteigaria 112
Marquise da Mobler 109
Mercado Campo Ourique 114
Mirari 114
Mu Gelato 113
Nannarella 113
Neighbourhood 112
O Velho Eurico 116
Panda Cantina 116
Pastéis de Belém 113
Pastéis de Nata 112
Páteo 13 119
Ponto Final 123
Rocco 124
Rosamar 126
Santini 113
Santo Lisboa, El 121
Seagull Method 109
Taberna Sal Grosso 116
Taqueria Paloma 123
Tasca Pete 119
Time Out Market 114
UAIPI Bebida e comida Brasiliera 110
Zé de Mouraria 119
Zero Zero 119

GOING OUT 128
A Baiuca 130
Bairro Alto 138
Bicaense 140
Black Sheep 135
Cante de Poeta 131
Casa Independente 140
Cave de Estrela 135
Clube de Fado 130
Clubs 138
Cocktails 136
Esplanada de Graça 131
Fábrica Braço de Prata 137
Fado 130
Finalmente Club 141
Foxtrot 136
Holy Wine 136
Kissaten, The 137
Lisbon Rio 139
Lost in 136
Lux Frágil 140
Mesa de Frades 130
Monsantos Open Air 140
MusicBox Lisboa 139
Palivlhão Chinês 136
Park Bar 137
Pensão de Amor 139
Queer 141
Quiosque da Riberia das Naus 135
Red Frog, The 138
Rua Cor-de-Rosa (Pink Street) 139
Secret Garden LX 134
Secret Poets Society 137
Tasca do Chico 130

Tasca do Jaime 131
Tribe Social Club 138
Trumps 141
Vino Vero 134
Wine 131

SHOPPING 142
How to dress like a local 144
Affordable Art & Home Deco 166
Art Supplies 164
Bookshops 160
Fashion & Department Stores 156
Flea Markets 146
Shops We Love 170
Streetwear 154
Vintage & second-hand 148
Vinyl & CDs 168

GREEN LISBON 172
Parks and swimming 174

Vegetarian and vegan Lisbon 179
Ao 26 – Vegan Food Project 179
Eight – The Health Lounge 182
Food Temple, The 181
Gaya Veggie Market 182
Green Affair, The 183
Jardim das Cerejas 179
Kong – Legumi Sushi 182
Manjerica 179
My Mother's Daughters 181
O Botanista 182
Organi Chiado 181
PSI 181
Vegan Junkies 182

OUTSIDE OF LISBON 184
Cascais 184
Comporta 184
Costa da Caparica & Sesimbra 185
Ericeira 185
Óbidos 186
Portinho da Arrábida & Galapinhos Beach 186
Sintra 186

ABOUT THE AUTHOR

Ana Kuijpers is a travel content creator who's half Portuguese and half Dutch. She lived in Portugal until she was 12, and since then, she's returned every year, not just to visit family but also to explore every corner of her home country. Even though she's originally from Porto, Lisbon holds a special place in her heart.

She returns to Lisbon whenever she can, drawn by its perfect mix: the good weather, the light in the city that just hits differently, the rich food culture, incredible beaches nearby, and the discoveries waiting to be made. She also loves how close Lisbon is to her favourite Portuguese region, Alentejo. There's no city like Lisbon, and it's Ana's favourite European capital. No matter how often she visits, the experience feels new yet familiar and comforting, like coming home.

WHY SHOULD I GO TO LISBON
the city you definitely need to visit
before you turn 30 (or 130)

Published in 2025 by
mo'media Rotterdam,
The Netherlands, momedia.nl

Concept
mo'media

Text and address selection
Ana Kuijpers

Art direction and illustration design
Jelle F. Post

Editing
Ezra van Wilgenburg, Maaike van Steekelenburg

Special thanks to
Tosca Bego, Iris Brans

Photography
Vincent van den Hoogen

All rights reserved. No part of this publication may be copied, displayed, extracted, reproduced, utilised, stored in a retrieval system or transmitted in any form or by any means, electronic, mechanical or otherwise including but not limited to photocopying, recording, or scanning without the prior written permission of the publisher.

 Copyright © mo'media BV, 2025

Why Should I Go To Lisbon
ISBN 978 94 9333 868 5
NUR 510

Disclaimer
The points of interested mentioned in this travel guide have been selected by the author. None of them have been paid for inclusion in this book: the *Why Should I Go To* book series is entirely ad-free.

Publisher's Note
Every effort has been made to ensure that the information in this book is accurate at the time of going to press. The publisher welcomes any information or suggestions for correction or improvement. Please send us an e-mail at info@momedia.nl.

 whyshouldigoto

WHY SHOULD I GO TO?
Information on all our travel guides
on **WHYSHOULDIGOTO.COM**

Why Should I Go To travel guides are available for the following cities: Amsterdam, Antwerp, Barcelona, Berlin, Budapest, Copenhagen, Dublin, London, Paris, Prague, Rome, Rotterdam, and Valencia. More cities will be added soon.